SAMUEL SCOWC
DIARY

Joan Francis

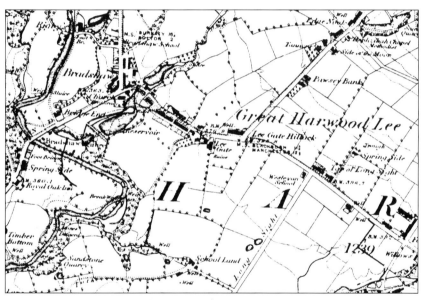

Map of Bradshaw Chapel and Longsight, Harwood.

Publication No. 26   September 2005

No 26 Samuel Scowcroft's Diary
Joan Francis
Published by Turton Local History Society,
September 2005
ISBN 1-904974-26-0

TURTON LOCAL HISTORY SOCIETY

Turton Local History Society exists to promote an interest in history by discussion, research and record. It is particularly concerned with the history of the old Urban District of Turton, Lancashire and its constituent ancient townships of Bradshaw, Edgworth, Entwistle, Harwood, Longworth, Quarlton and Turton.

This publication is the twenty sixth issued by the Society. A list of previous publications is given on the inside front cover.

Meetings of the Society are held from September to May inclusive, beginning at 7.30 pm on the third Tuesday of each month at the Barlow Institute, Edgworth. Visitors are welcome.

ILLUSTRATIONS

AUTHOR'S NOTE ON THE SCOWCROFT FAMILY

Since the mid 1700s, the Scowcroft family has been influential in Bradshaw, Harwood and Bolton in general. None more so that Samuel Scowcroft's branch of the family, who were involved in the building of the schools and churches that form the fabric of Bradshaw and Harwood as they are today.

James Lee, who was a great uncle to Samuel Scowcroft, originally started the Scowcroft diary in 1814. When Samuel took over he continued to record events of personal, local, regional and even national interest over a period of fifty years that finally ended in 1914.

Fortunately for local historians the 'Scowcroft Diaries' passed through the family to Samuel's granddaughter, the late Miss Mary Scowcroft, who preserved them and made them available for this study.

ACKNOWLEDGEMENTS

Mary Scowcroft (Harwood) for the extended loan of the Scowcroft Diaries and related documents over many years.

Arthur Critchley (Canada), an ex-Harwood man and member of the Scowcroft family, for his gift to the Society of a computerized breakdown of information in the diaries.

Bolton Evening News for photographs and reports

James J Francis (Bradshaw) for arranging the illustrations

Mary E Riley (Bradshaw) for the tedious preparation of the script

The many people of Bradshaw and Harwood who, over many years, have loaned photographs of great local interest.

SAMUEL SCOWCROFT
1838-1914

The story of the Diarist

This is a brief biography of Samuel Scowcroft, the author of the now famous 'Scowcroft Diaries' the contents of which have been invaluable to local historians and genealogists around the world. The first entries were from a diary started by James Lee of Brookfold Lane dated 1814 and continued by his son Thomas, then passed to Samuel Scowcroft who began his diaries in 1861. There have been many Scowcrofts in Bradshaw and Harwood over the centuries, a number of them being notable figures in local society, including farmers, publicans, colliery owners and managers.

Grandfather

Samuel was descended from John Scowcroft, his grandfather, who was born at Ruins, Harwood on the 21st December 1777 and baptized at Bolton Parish Church on the 15th February 1778. He was described as a weaver when he married Martha Haslam on the 20th July 1800 at Bolton Parish Church. They had eleven children and lived as tenant farmers at Springside Farm, Harwood in 1841, later moving to Scowcroft Houses, Ruins Lane, Harwood in 1851. By 1861 they lived at Middle of the Moor Harwood.

John was a trustee of Harwood Wesleyan School when teetotalism, the total abstinence from alcohol, came to Harwood on the 29th May 1835. The first meeting of the Harwood Temperance Society was held at Harwood Wesleyan School and John was the first person to sign the pledge, becoming a founder member of the Society. In 1837 John was the first elected Guardian of the Poor for Bradshaw Township. He was a very strict and religious person all his life and when he appeared in the Harwood Wesleyan School and thumped his stick on the floor there was an immediate silence and complete order.

Father

John's eldest son Samuel was the father of Samuel the diarist. Samuel married Jane Bolton of Harwood at Bolton Parish Church on the 18th July 1817 when they were 20 and 17 respectively. Samuel and Jane had six children; John born 1818, Sophia 1822, Richard 1827, Sarah 1831, Martha 1834 who died as a young child and Samuel Junior born 15th September 1838. The youngest son became the author of the diaries which he kept for nearly 50 years.

John Scowcroft (1777-1862). The Diarist's Grandfather.

St Peter Parish Church of Bolton–le-Moors. 1860.
Early Scowcrofts were baptised, married and buried here.

Son

The first cottages on Bradshaw Road and the realignment of Lee Gate were completed in 1838 and Samuel was born in one of the newly built cottages on Bradshaw Road. He was a child born into the Victorian era supposedly seen and not heard. Samuel was only an hour old when his father enrolled him in the Harwood Temperance Society, his father and grandfather already being members; his mother was the first woman to sign.

Bradshaw was well placed for schools, as within walking distance of the Bradshaw Chapel area, Samuel's home, there were two, Bradshaw School founded 1807, at the corner of Rigby Lane, now known as 'The Old Post Office' and Harwood Wesleyan School founded 1822. Well schooled in reading, writing and arithmetic, his early education shows through in his entries of local, regional and national news, his well-written diary and his capability of running the family grocery business. He later became a man of property.

When Samuel was 3 years old his sister Sophia married James Roscow at Bolton Parish Church, there were five children from this marriage. The year following, his brother John married Alice Morris of Turton, also at Bolton Parish Church. Alice unfortunately died in 1843 after the birth of their only child Edwin and a year later John married Hannah Frodsham, his second wife, at Bolton Parish Church.

School

In 1843 it was time for Samuel to go to school. It is probable that he went to the Harwood Wesleyan School, as the family were staunch Wesleyan Methodists. For his first day at school his mother would have bought him new clogs, which became his pride and joy with their shiny toecaps. Samuel walked to school with his friends along Lee Gate and Longsight hoping to be clean and tidy by the time they arrived. The master was very strict about arriving with clean hands and footwear, no mud had to be brought into the school, although the floors were stone flags. A sharp rap on the knuckles with a cane punished any disobedience or excuses. The teacher's favourite pupils were expected to help by filling inkwells, carrying the register and by giving out books, paper and quills, later pen nibs and holders. The children were also expected to attend Sunday school where they continued with their Bible Studies. Lighting was supplied by oil lamps and candles, while the room was warmed by a coal or coke-burning stove.

Samuel was a keen scholar and quite happy to go to school, not playing truant like some boys, or having to take his father's dinner to work as many children

Springside Farm C.1940 off Longsight. Built post Enclosure 1797 and tenanted by John Scowcroft 1841

Bradshaw School founded 1807, used as a Post Office when the new St Maxentius School was built in 1880.

Harwood Wesleyan School founded in 1822

The Bradshaw Road cottage, completed in 1838. where Samuel Scowcroft was born 15th Sept 1838.

The Bradshaw blacksmith's shop in the basement of the old Lee Gate Bleachworks building – now the Conservative Club.

were expected to. Children who travelled quite a distance and didn't go home for dinner would take bread and cheese to eat with a drink of water. On the homeward journey when clean hands were not essential Samuel and his friend would visit his grandfather at Springside Farm, Harwood. They would help to fill up hay racks and do any other small jobs hoping they had earned a drink of milk, then it would be a mad dash to the blacksmith's at Lee Gate to see if there were any horses waiting to be shod. After that it would be home for tea. Samuel was one of the lucky ones who were well fed, having a working father and living at a grocer's shop.

Leisure

Leisure time would be spent fishing in Bradshaw Brook and Riding Gate Brook; making their own rods from sticks, string and a pin, no expensive tackle in those days for children. They also loved to dam the streams to make deeper pools for wading; another favourite game was walking the plank over the stream at Labby's Walk Mill. Amongst their other activities were sailing pieces of paper or wood under Bradshaw Bridge, which sowed the seed for Samuel's future love of sailing.

Their most enjoyable pastime was going to Lawrence Horrocks the blacksmith to watch him using the bellows on the coals to make them glow red-hot before he could start making horseshoes. There was always the sound of the hammer on the anvil, the smell of leather and smoking coals. Horses were taken to the blacksmith's regularly as they would often lose a shoe or need a new set. The blacksmith would make spare shoes ready for the horses that were regular visitors; these would be hung on racks and named. Sometimes Samuel would help his parents and when all the chores were finished he would be allowed out to roam the area with his friends creating their own exciting adventures.

It was a very sad day for the family on the 12th January 1846 when grandmother Martha Scowcroft died. She was a very kind and capable woman who was greatly missed, especially by Samuel who being seven years old liked to visit his grandparents at Springside Farm.

When Samuel's brother Richard was 23 in 1849, he married Lucinda Booth at Deane Parish Church. Unfortunately after only four years of marriage Lucinda died in 1853 leaving a daughter Jane who went to live at Bradshaw Chapel with her grandparents.

On leaving school Samuel started work as an errand boy in his uncle's shop, learning the grocery trade and becoming a shop assistant.

Birth of the Grocery Business

The family grocery business was started by his mother Jane about 1845. It is alleged that her husband Samuel came home from work one day and told her that a man had died suddenly leaving a wife and young family without any means of support. Jane was asked by her son Samuel what she would do in the same circumstances; her quick reply was 'start a business'. Without further promptings she purchased a few bottles of sweets, arranged them on shelves in the front room of the cottage on Bradshaw Road and a new shop was born. Her husband Samuel was still a timekeeper but later when the shop was established, he joined his wife in the grocery business. The shop was named ' Samuel Scowcroft', licensed to sell tea and tobacco.

Samuel as a teenager

Samuel, having a great interest in current events, at the early age of thirteen went to watch Prince Albert with the Duke of Wellington riding in their carriage from Barrow Bridge Mills to Bolton. They rode down Chorley Old Road into Bridge Street where Samuel was waiting in the crowd to cheer them on their way. In December 1855 another important event took place in Bolton, the opening of the new Market Hall and Samuel was once again in the crowds watching. Later when Samuel became a well-known figure in Bradshaw Society he would receive many special invitations to local events, which he duly recorded in his diary.

When Samuel's sister Sarah was 24 years old in 1855, she married William Laithwaite at Bolton Parish Church who later became an important figure at the Harwood Wesleyan Chapel. By this time all Samuel's brothers and sisters were married leaving only Samuel at home on Bradshaw Road with his parents.

The Grocer's Shop

When the family business had become more prosperous, Samuel joined his parents, as he was now a capable shopkeeper. Customers coming into the shop would give him information on the health of friends, any accidents, deaths or suicides; the grocery shop became a huge source of knowledge and gossip. This information prompted him to start his own recordings in 1861; he wrote in notebooks, exercise books on pieces of paper and eventually in diaries, unfortunately some periods were mislaid.

It wasn't all doom and gloom in Bradshaw, in April 1861 one happy occasion occurred when brother Richard, a widower married his second wife Catherine Crompton at Bradshaw Church. Soon after, Samuel senior retired, leaving his

Barrow Bridge Mills visited by Prince Albert and the Duke of Wellington,
Oct 11th 1851 and seen by young Samuel.

Samuel was present at the opening ceremony of Bolton's new Market Hall,
Dec 17th 1855

Extract. from James Lee's book of Brookfold, Harwood
dated apl 6.
1812
1814

Bolton Riot apl 20 1812

Prime Minister was shot May 11th 1812 (his life, he lived till over 80 years 92)
Saml Lee (Sam & Charles) was shot March 11th 1824. (not killed but bore the marks all)
Mr. Sadler rose from Bolton (in a balloon) Sep 29th 1824 and was killed

Charles Lee died apl 17th 1829 aged 76 left 7 sons and four

daughters 72 Grand children and 28 great grandchildren,
Oer. 15th 1822 James Bolton Lent Nifty Lee 1 guiney (24-)
April 25th 1827 Great Snow fall
augt 2nd 1827 Thomas Lee & James Scholes Sailed to Ireland
July 1828 Great Flood

Power Looms was broken at Ramsbottom, and ten
Morgan
Men and one Killed apl 26th 1826.
Turks fleet was taken oct 20th 1827
Quel between the Duke of Wellington and the Earl
Winchester 21 March 1829
March 1st 1829
32 lives lost at Hide (Hyde) ‖ Manchester Riot 400 power
Looms burnt March 4th 1829
John Horridge Kild James Bromily, March 20th 1829
York Minster was burnt Feby 2nd 1829 50 000 pounds
Mill Hill (Bolton) factory was burnt Jany 21st 1829.
Longsight school was built in 1822
New War with Portagale and 10,000 men sald Dec 1815 1826
New Railway was opened augt 1st 1828 at Bolton
New Railway was opened between Liverpool and
Manchester sept 15th 1830.
Bradshaw Workes oct 2 4th and 6th 1828.
July 7th 1823 First stone was laid at Bolton Trinity church
July 27. 1825 Hardcastle stove was burnt
August 16th 1819. Manchester fight

*The first page of the Diary, comprising extracts from the previous
diary of James Lee of Brookfold Lane, Harwood. James was an uncle of
Samuel Scowcroft's mother.*

Hall James Barker was wounded and died sept 30/47 (they were celebrating John Cross wedding. and shooting with 5lb weight when they were ramming one of these with a iron bar the weight burst with the above result *JL*)

Oct 20th 1848 Power Looms first gated in Harwood by Zechariah Nuttall. *on Brookside between Ruins & Hardy Mill Road*

Nov 8 1849 Wesley Chapel Bolton First Stone was Laid.

Jany 1850 The Expedition in search of sir Franklin. the Enterprise. Captn Collinson Commander

March 1st 1850 Thomas Marsden was drowned in Bradshaw Hall lodge *SS*

(my father went to Skipton to inform his brother Dr Marsden of the above)

Apl 12th 1850 Robert Lomax died aged 53 years

May 14. 1851 Ralph Pilling died *at sea* and was buried at Bradshaw Chapel (Church) June 2nd in a lead Coffin (died at sea coming from US)

July 11th 1851 New Wesley Chapel Bradshawgate was opened

Sep 17th 1851 Charles Hopwood was Married (Ellen Ormrod)

Oct 10th 1851 Queen Victoria came to Manchester

Oct 11th 1851 Prince Albert came to Bolton (I saw the Prince also the Duke of Wellington. sat with him in the carraige they had been to Barrow Bridge Mills)

March 18. 1852 West Scowcroft *astonus Farm* died aged 72 (my fathers Uncle)

July 13. 1852 Star Hinn (Inn) burnt down Churchgate Bolton

Augt 8' 1856 *Thomas Jolly* Cut his Childrens throat, x his own. (7 Stars row)

augt 10th 1852 Rushford Bridge left Harwood for New York (Jn Rumsey wife & family)

Sep 16 1855 Thomas Scowcroft died aged 72 (John father Bradshaw Chapel) *buried Branch*

Sep 10 1855 Sabestepol Taken

Dec 17 1855 Bolton New Market (Hall) place was opened

Febry 25 1856 Robert Bolton was Married (cous in Robt)

1852 First Stone Laid for New Factory Nab Brow in Hugh Gillibrand field

James Lee's entries 1848-1856. Includes a note of Prince Albert's visit to Bolton and Barrow Bridge and another about Zachariah Nuttall's power looms in the Ruins area and of the new factory at Nab Brow (Prospect Mill).

*An early photograph of a Longsight Wesleyan School
Class. c.1890.*

*The new Wesleyan Chapel
opened Friday Nov 21st 1862.*

sons Samuel and Richard as partners in the business. The shop became 'Samuel Scowcroft and Sons', licensed to sell tea and tobacco. On his retirement Samuel Snr. became interested in buying property - he purchased six houses in Apple Street, Bolton, four houses in Leegate and various other properties.

The family were greatly saddened on New Year's Day in 1862 when Grandfather John Scowcroft died at Longsight aged 84. All the family respected him and missed his sound advice. Unfortunately he didn't live long enough to see how well his grandson did in business and in his footsteps as Trustee for the chapel, Overseer for Harwood and Guardian for Bradshaw.

Letters from America were the highlights of those days. Samuel's mother received them from her uncle, James Bolton of New York and other relatives who had left England in the early 1800's. The family would gather together and wait with anticipation to hear them read aloud by their mother and listen to tales of that wonderful country called America. Some Bradshaw families received gifts of a few cents or even dollars.

Samuel allowed himself days off from his business for special events, as it wasn't all work and no play. On one such occasion on 24th September 1862 he went to Bolton to watch the unveiling of Samuel Crompton's statue in Nelson Square. It was a gala day with processions, hundreds of people in the streets, with a grand concert in the evening, altogether a very exciting day full of life and laughter. One of the first photographs in the Bolton Evening News was of this event.

New Wesleyan Chapel

A most important occasion in Harwood occurred on Friday 21st November 1862 when the new Wesleyan Chapel was opened by the Reverend John Hannah. The church was full for both afternoon and evening celebrations, which was a very pleasing sight. On Sunday the normal services were continued and very importantly an excellent collection was taken. Samuel being a businessman noted very carefully the collections taken at Harwood Wesleyan Chapel as well as at Bradshaw Church.

Samuel had to keep his eyes on his business as well as the church, the school and affairs of the area. In 1862, during the American Civil War, supplies of cotton to Lancashire mills became restricted, causing short time working, unemployment, misery and poverty. The Harwood Wesleyan Chapel trustees called a committee meeting to discuss what could be done to help and on their behalf Samuel opened a shop at Castle Hill to provide food and clothing at low prices. In charge of the shop were Timothy Pollitt and Richard Greenhalgh. The

*The unveiling of the statue of Samuel Crompton, the inventor of the Spinning
Mule, which Samuel Scowcroft attended on 24th September 1862.*

*The corner shop at Bradshaw Chapel where young
Samuel learned his trade with his uncle.*

A painting of Bradshaw Chapel c.1870, in the possession of Mary Scowcroft.

A view of the Bradshaw Road cottages from the top of the Chapel Tower.
Samuel's shop is No 76 next to the corner property No 74.

local relief lasted for three years during which Mr James Hardcastle of Bradshaw Hall provided 1000 tons of coal to be distributed to the poor. At this period the Hardcastles had collieries at Hill End, Harwood and Breightmet.

Liverpool Docks

With the advent of the railways, Samuel was able to travel further afield. One day in 1863 he took the train to Liverpool to see the ships in the Mersey. What a sight to delight the eye, the Great Eastern steamship was in dock, quite different from Samuel's dreams when he sailed his paper boats under Bradshaw Bridge. He was so enthralled with the docks that he made another visit when once again the Great Eastern was in port as well as two men-of-war, the Majestic and Liverpool, a wondrous sight. Samuel was a confident young man of 25 and he spoke to the seamen who told him tales of the horrors of gales, rough seas, poor food and the wonders of far away lands. The port was full of activity, ships being loaded and unloaded, smells of spices and perfumes from the Far East but no cotton bales from America, some cotton from India but of an inferior quality; he also watched a ship in the dry dock being repaired.

A number of Scowcroft relatives had sailed from Liverpool to live in America and Canada, so these visits became sentimental journeys. Samuel loved the bustle, activity and smell of the sea, he would have loved to sail away in one of the ships but his grocery business and his parents needed him. Samuel returned home with dreams and wonderful memories but by the time he had arrived home in Bradshaw he was back down to earth and ready for his everyday duties.

1863 Now legal shop owner

Samuel worked with Richard until 1863 when Richard decided to leave the business to open a shop of his own further up Bradshaw Road, leaving Samuel as the sole owner at No 76. The dissolution of the partnership was processed legally, signed on 8th May 1863 and advertised in the London Gazette on 12th May. By this date Samuel senior, his wife Jane and son Samuel were still at the family home in Bradshaw Chapel.

As Samuel's business became busier he decided he needed a horse and cart and on 16th December 1863 went to a farm sale at Brown Barn, Bradshaw. There is always lots of excitement and sadness at a farm sale, Samuel had a good look round at the stock and saw a horse that would be excellent for his needs for which he paid £20 and 10 shillings. He called the horse Diamond; a faithful friend for 26 years and it was a sad day when he died in November 1889.

*Brother Richard's shop at the end of the second terrace of the
Bradshaw Road cottages.*

*Brown Barn Farm where Samuel bought his horse 'Diamond
at the auction on 16th Dec 1863.*

Many children died when quite young in Victorian times, as medicine was not so advanced as today. Before Christmas 1863 his sister Sarah Anne's nine-month-old baby died of a fever. That Christmas was not a joyful one for the family who spent a quiet time together.

The affairs of the Harwood Wesleyan Chapel are noted when the trustees decided at a committee meeting to hire a harmonium for six months at a cost of 30 shillings a quarter. Then Mr William Laithwaite, Samuel's brother-in-law, generously decided to buy an Alexander harmonium for the chapel. It was appreciated by the congregation as shown by the first collection, which was quite a considerable amount.

Samuel, becoming a prominent figure in Bradshaw, was invited to many official ceremonies. At the opening of Farnworth Park in September 1864 by Mr Gladstone, Samuel was there with his girlfriend Elizabeth, it being a very auspicious occasion with all the local dignitaries in attendance.

Another exciting event occurred a few months later in Bradshaw when gas was piped to the houses in Bradshaw Chapel and Samuel had it installed in his shop, which was a great improvement on oil lamps and candles.

Samuel needed to be diplomatic especially when the Bolton postmaster Mr Davidson asked him to have the sub post office in his grocery store. Up to that time it had been in James Chadwick's shop at Bradshaw Chapel, and Samuel started a successful petition to keep it there. James Chadwick was a shoemaker and a much respected church clerk and sexton when he became the sub postmaster. By then he was already an old man and Samuel thought he would soon be retiring but he remained sub postmaster until three months before his death on 11th January 1873 at the age of 80. During his time as postmaster an afternoon delivery was introduced; the twice-daily service commencing on 25th April 1864. Later Samuel's brother Richard ran the sub post office from his business in Bradshaw Road. During this busy period in his life, Samuel established a pattern of recording the interesting local happenings as well as regional and national events in his diaries.

Marriage

As Samuel's business was prospering he decided it was time to marry his sweetheart. On 16th May 1865 he married Elizabeth Haslam of Tong Fields, Dunscar at Walmsley Church; the service was taken by Reverend Christopher Cronshaw, curate of St Georges, Bolton. The couple returned to Bradshaw Chapel to live – no mention of a honeymoon in his diary, it was back to work.

Walmsley Church where Samuel married Elizabeth Haslam of Tong Fields on 16th May 1865.

The Boot & Clogmakers' shop of T. Bridge in Bradshaw Chapel adjacent to the 'Crofters Arms'. Note the attached cottage to the left, now demolished. c.1910.

1872

Jan 27/72 Thos. Bolton (alias Tom oaten) Marr'd to Mary Ann Ramsden

Jan 29/72 John Bolton Bridge Marr'd to Sarah Allen at Bridge St. Wesleyan Chapel by Rev Hy Hartling

Jan 26/72 Alice Brown wife of Rich'd Brown and Mary Brown daughter of
Richard and Alice Brown taken to Fishpool work house

Feby 4/72 Alice Brown wife of Rich'd Brown died aged 46 at Fishpool

Feby 3/72 Mary wife of Jos. Allen del'd of a son

Feby 8 Alice wife of Rich'd Brown interred at Wes Chapel Harwood

Feby 8 Robert Rogerson died at Firwood fold aged 19

Feb 9 Frank Weaver took up for stealing a watch at Dutton field (Nathan Ramsden works)

Feby 11 Rich'd Roscoe of Bolton and Eliz Darbyshire of Farnworth Marr'd at Emanuel Ch Bolton

Feby 12 Frank Weaver of Longsight and a youth McQuaries were committed for
trial for stealing a watch belonging to Wm Rothwell from the
Works of Nathan Ramsden. Bleacher. Harwood

Feby 10/72 Thomas Kershaw for asaulting a young woman at Darwen was
Sent to prison for Six Months . Thos Kershaw of Bradshaw

Feby 21/72 About four oclock Miss Galindo was knocked down and
run over by a cart belonging to Jane Hall, publican and
Brewer of Eagley Bridge . at Bradshaw Chapel. her Leg was badly
broken. We took her home to Oaks station road in Jethro Scowcroft trap.

Feby 24/72 At the Bolton Parish Ch Thos Gresty to Alice Booth both of Little Lever.

 "/72 James Howarth (Betty Bumpers) Leegate died

- 24/72 Joseph Howarth Side of Moor died

 " 11/72 Wm Miller (alias Peastick) died aged 32

 " 14/72 Robert Robinson Farmer Davenport Farm Harwood
Committed suicide by hanging himself in the shippon near to
the house . was hung in a kneeling position. The nail to which
he was hung was only about three feet from the ground .
A very quiet decent man. He marr'd Abigal Brooks of Leegate

*Diary entries during 1872. The July 21st entry details an early 'traffic'
accident when Miss Galindo, the sister of the Bradshaw vicar,
Rev Galindo, was run over by a cart.*

Samuel and Elizabeth had four children – Edith, Samuel, Peter Alfred and Robert Bolton. Their first child Edith was born on 30th January 1866, and she became Samuel's favourite, probably because she was the only girl and the boys had stronger personalities like their father. Their second child, born in 1868, was named Samuel, a well used family name. The birth was celebrated quietly at home and with prayers in the chapel.

The trustees of Harwood Wesleyan Chapel each year organised the sermons, concerts and other activities. These were all well attended with excellent collections taken; this money went towards the every day running of the chapel and to help with future developments, the following decision being a good example. At a special meeting of the committee it was decided that with the growth in numbers of the congregation, side galleries should be erected in the chapel and these were opened on 9th June 1867.

In 1871 the trustees decided to appoint a new schoolmaster for the Harwood Wesleyan School and a tea party was organised by Samuel who introduced Mr Alfred Booth to the committee. He was to start teaching on 9th January 1871, it being his first appointment on finishing at Westminster Training College. He was obviously a good and well respected master as he stayed thirty-nine years except for a short period at Darcy Lever Wesleyan School.

New Shop

As Samuel's grocery business was booming, he started preparing for a new shop and storeroom to expand the sales, as well as adding a drapery section. The site was on the opposite side of Bradshaw Road between the Crofters Arms and Rigby Lane. He was able to watch the builders at work, making sure they did everything according to the plans; the family moved into the shop on completion in 1871. The stone buildings are still there today and are currently being converted into apartments.

Samuel was a prominent figure in Bradshaw and Harwood being on the chapel and school committees and a well-known shopkeeper. The villagers came to respect his opinion and would call into the shop where he was easily accessible to discuss any problems. Any accidents at Bradshaw Chapel and Samuel was on the scene to help. One such occasion was when the sister of the Reverend Galindo, vicar at Bradshaw Church was knocked down and run over by a cart belonging to Jane Hall, Publican and Brewer of Eagley Bridge, and her leg badly broken. Samuel, ever resourceful, borrowed Jethro Scowcroft's trap and took Miss Galindo to her home at The Oaks, Station Road, now 'Rockwood' on Oaks Lane, Bradshaw. On other occasions he went with Doctor Crompton to identify bodies found in the river, the reservoir or abandoned in the churchyard;

most he recognised but sometimes it was a complete mystery. One winter he made a raft to retrieve the body of a young boy who had fallen through the ice on the reservoir behind St Maxentius Church.

Walsh's Educational Institute

When David Walsh, the last miller of Hardy Corn Mill died in 1847, he left all his estate to Charles James Darbyshire with the intention of establishing a charity trusteeship. It took 20 years before the trustees met in Bank Street Chapel in 1867 to propose the construction of a building for use as a school, public library and reading room for the general education of the inhabitants of Harwood and the neighbourhood. In 1872 the grand edifice was finished and opened in May. A poster was displayed in Harwood, which read: -

Walsh's Educational Institution, Harwood.
The Inaugural soiree of the above named Institution will be held on Saturday 4th May 1872 in the lecture hall of the Institution. Tea on the tables at 5 pm. Chair to be taken at 6 pm by John Harwood Esq. JP.

Tickets eight pence each may be had from the Provisional Committee or at the entrance to the Institution. Short addresses will be delivered by other Friends of the Institution and of education generally. Vocal music will be given by a select choir assisted by Mr Councillor Bromiley of Bolton. Readings will also be given by Messrs John Harwood and John Scoles of Manchester. Members will be enrolled during the evening.

Robert Kenyon, General Printer, Market Street, Bolton.

Samuel, his family and many of his relatives would attend the tea party, as they were all very supportive of all the concerts and entertainment in the area. One wonders how many people would have been able to read the poster? The grocery shop became very busy as the population of the locality continued to grow and Samuel found it necessary to employ an assistant. His brother John's son, Abel Scowcroft was found to be suitable and was employed in the shop. With a very capable assistant, Samuel could now visit his other shops and take occasional holidays.

The New Bradshaw Church

There was always lots of activity in Bradshaw, the new Parish Church was completed and the consecration of the church was held on 9th November 1872 by the Lord Bishop of Manchester, Dr Fraser. A pavilion at Bridge End was erected to celebrate the event and 1500 tickets at one shilling each were sold for a public lunch. Many other dignitaries were there including the vicar of Bolton,

Walsh's Institute built by the Trustees of the Estate of David Walsh, the last miller of Hardy Corn Mill, in 1872.

Thomas Hardcastle and Jethro Scowcroft who all made speeches. Samuel was in charge of the carving of the beef, a very important job, to cut sufficient slices for 1500 plates. It was a hugely successful day enjoyed by everyone.

A few weeks later on Christmas Day 1872 there was a wedding in the family, when brother Richard's daughter Jane, who had lived with the family after her mother's death, was married to Mark Millington at Bradshaw Old Church by Reverend Galindo. It was one of the last weddings in the old Church building before closure and demolition; the first marriage in the new Church was in April 1873.

Many meetings were held in the new pavilion at Bridge End, which Samuel usually attended. One of the meetings concerned starting a rifle corps; another involved moving the Township meetings from the Britannia Inn to Walsh's Institute. This was the first attempt to move meetings away from public houses; it was finally authorised in March 1874 to the satisfaction of the teetotallers. After a meeting to form a rifle corps organised by a Captain, Adjutant Frances and a drill sergeant, a rifle range was constructed near Bradshaw Bridge.

BRADSHAW CHURCH.

THE NEW CHURCH WILL (D.V.) BE

CONSECRATED

BY THE

LORD BISHOP OF MANCHESTER,

On Saturday, November 9th, 1872.

DIVINE SERVICE TO COMMENCE AT 11 O'CLOCK.

After Service there will be

A PUBLIC LUNCH

AT TWO O'CLOCK (D.V.),

IN A PAVILION NEAR THE CHURCH.

THE RIGHT REV.

The Lord Bishop of Manchester

Has kindly consented to Speak.

Tickets of admission to the Service will be presented to the holders of Sittings in the New Church; and if there should be any to spare they may be obtained by the Public from the PARISH CLERK.

Tickets for the Lunch (limited to 1,500), price One Shilling each, may be obtained by Parishioners from the PARISH CLERK, on and after MONDAY NEXT, OCTOBER 21, till the end of the week, after which time any Tickets remaining unsold may be procured by the Public from Mr. BRADBURY, Stationer, Deansgate, Bolton.

The Clergy are requested to wear Surplices, and to assemble in the Vestry, at 10-30.

The Chancel will be reserved for the Clergy and the Choir.

The notice inviting Bradshaw Parishioners to the Bradshaw Church Consecration Lunch at the large Pavilion, newly built on Bolton Road between Bridge End House and the Bradshaw Brook.

New Organ for Wesleyan Chapel

Walsh's Institute also became a centre of entertainments, the first tea party being in May 1873. Two more concerts were held to raise money for the purchase of a new organ for Harwood Wesleyan Chapel, both were excellent performances making a good profit. In January 1875 the trustees had made sufficient funds to order a new organ. Samuel went with his uncle John Bolton and William Laithwaite to James Cole's organ works at Cornbrook, Manchester, to oversee the organ being built. The cost quoted was £235; after discussion they decided they needed an extra stop, the oboe. Joseph Tootill, William Laithwaite and Samuel agreed they would share the cost of the extra component.

Time came for Samuel to have a day off and there was no better way to spend it than to go to the unveiling of Dr Chadwick's statue in Bolton Town Hall Square on 1st August 1873. He never let any of these important events pass him by and enjoyed being among throngs of people. He was stimulated by the excitement and seriousness of the occasion and the fact that these important events happened in his town. The next invitation Samuel received was in July 1874 when the cornerstone was laid for the new Birtenshaw chapel by Alderman Peter Crook Marsden. It was attended by all the local dignitaries.

Samuel was involved with both the Wesleyan Chapel and Bradshaw Church and different means of raising money had to be organised. In February 1874 there was a sale in the Pavilion of china cups and saucers with a print of Bradshaw Old Church on them; these china pieces can still be found in antique shops. The Pavilion became a popular venue for entertainments, presentations, meetings and tea parties. Today there isn't a sign of the building.

Although Bradshaw and Harwood were small villages, there were always lots of entertainment, unusual events, births, deaths, marriages and even fires. One fire broke out in February 1874 in the attic of the blacksmith's house in Bradshaw Chapel, occupied by Thomas Briggs. There was no fire brigade in those days and they depended on the fire appliances kept at Bradshaw Works. On this occasion the fire engine brought from Hardcastle's was called the 'Water Witch', it was quite a distance for a horse drawn or man hauled vehicle when your house was burning fiercely. Until it arrived, villagers would have doused the fire with buckets of water, which would be carried from Riding Gate Brook or the reservoir at Lee Gate. Samuel was always in the centre of the activity organising and controlling the volunteers.

*One of the China saucers sold with cups to raise money
towards the cost of the new Church.*

*The new St. Maxentius Church, consecrated on 9th Nov 1872.
The old chapel had previously been demolished except for the tower which
was retained as a monument.*

Changes in Bradshaw

There was great rejoicing on Saturday 28th February 1874 when the toll bars between Bolton and Ramsbottom were dismantled and the gates and buildings were sold, much to Samuel's joy as he used to pay a toll every time his horse and cart went through, especially the Oaks Bar which he had to pass through to his shop on Tonge Moor Road or on his way to Bolton.

The following month was another happy time when Samuel's third child Peter Alfred was born. Mother and baby were both doing well but there was no mention of a christening party or presents. They would go to church later to give thanks for a safe delivery.

In May 1875, at Harwood Wesleyan School, a celebration tea party was given by Richard Tootill on his retirement as foreman at Bradshaw Works. He received some very generous gifts; Thomas Hardcastle presented him with a silver tea service with a £50 note in the teapot, an opera glass from the workmen and a Bible from his friends including Samuel. Mr John Holt acted as chairman and it was an impressive occasion.

The following year on 3rd February 1876, Samuel senior died at 76 Bradshaw Chapel. He was aged 78 and had enjoyed his retirement studying the property market, buying a few houses and participating in all the affairs of the church. He was buried in Bradshaw churchyard.

Samuel began to travel further afield, using the convenience of the railways he could be in London in a few hours, so off he went to the capital for a few days. He travelled alone so he could enjoy his own interests, which of course would include a visit to the docks to watch the ships being unloaded of their wonderful cargoes of spices, perfumes and more mundane goods and merchandise being loaded for far away lands. After some refreshment he would go to admire St Paul's Cathedral, Westminster Abbey, the Tower of London, the Houses of Parliament, Buckingham Palace and the various bridges across the Thames. At the end of his holiday he returned home full of the delights of London to regale his family with all he had seen. Elizabeth his wife hadn't been able to accompany him, as she was a little unwell owing to their fourth child being due in December. On 11th December 1877 their son Robert Bolton was born.

The following years were full of meetings, concerts, sermons, improvements to his business and new projects to raise money for the Longsight chapel and school. By 1880 the number of pupils on the school register had increased and the trustees met to discuss the possibility of a new school. Before they could demolish the old school, arrangements had to be made to rehouse the existing

1880   24/

Feb 24th Put the Bridge across the brook at Rigby's bought from Mr Henry Ashworth.

26th Buried Wellington Hargreaves

March 1st The Harwood Trs Trustees met at Wesly Chapel Revd Mr Marshall Randles in the Chair
agreed to accept Sherwood & Reverly architects of Manchester plan for new school
estimated to cost 1250£

March 2 Abraham Entwistle (Tom Noah's son) died of typ fever

„ 3 Saml Brooks (James son) discharged from Bradshaw works

„ 8 John Holt, Joseph Lovett & Ash Ashworth. staked 35 yds square of land out
including the present school (Mr Thomas Hardcastle having told John Southern to
mark out what was wanted last friday) for Mr J Hardcastle to see. he came up
to day. but Richd Lovett & me made it 40 yds from Longsight lane towards
the Hillock so that it was 40×35 yds. He (Mr S H) promised to give the land
marked out and also the present Ground rent of about /2-60 now being
paid. We were all very pleased at such a generous gift.
The building committee met this night at appointed Sherwood & Peverley
Architects (And at Mr Hardcastles suggestion to day Messrs Ashworths of Rose
Hill were ordered to make a plan of the land being conveyd to trustees)

March 17 Jethro Scowcroft (moorfield) died this afternoon about 2 o'clock
having been poorly about 4 months, of Tumor with cancer tendency.

March 21 Jethro Scowcroft. John Priestly's son born at Bradshaw Chapel.

„ 31 Chas Cooper (Bradshaw Chapel) Blacksmith died this
afternoon was buried at Edgworth Congregation Chapel Bradshaw Chl april 5th

„ 31 Bradshaw Township meeting. I was chairman

Diary entries for Feb-Mar 1880. The new footbridge at the Rigby's is noted as well as details of Thomas Hardcastle's gift of land for the Wesleyan School.

HARWOOD
WESLEYAN NEW SCHOOL.

On Saturday, June 26th, 1880,

THE

CORNER-STONE

OF THE ABOVE SCHOOL WILL BE LAID BY

THOMAS HARDCASTLE, ESQ.,

OF BRADSHAW HALL,

AT FOUR O'CLOCK IN THE AFTERNOON.

At Five o'clock a Public Tea will be provided in Walsh's Institute. Tickets 1/ each.

AFTER WHICH A

PUBLIC MEETING

Will be held in the WESLEYAN CHAPEL.

The scheme has the support of the following Ministers and Gentlemen, most of whom are expected to be present on the occasion :—

Rev. D. J. Waller.	P. C. Marsden, Esq. J.P.	Edmund Ashworth, Esq.
„ M. Randles.	George Knowles, Esq.	William Slater, Esq.
„ W. L. Watkinson.	W. W. Cannon, Esq. J.P.	Mr. Councillor Wood.
„ W. D. L. Slack.	Thomas Walker, Esq.	R. Spencer, Esq.
„ W. Cornforth.	Roger Haslam, Esq.	J. W. Brown, Esq.
„ Thomas Pennington.	T. L. Rushton, Esq. J.P.	Samuel Isherwood, Esq.
„ R. K. Judson.	J. F. Knowles, Esq.	Jas. Musgrave, Esq. jun.
„ C. B. Shirres.	Thomas Scowcroft, Esq.	Wm. Musgrave, Esq.
Thomas Hardcastle, Esq.	Jeremiah Garnett, Esq.	Yates Duxbury, Esq.
Richard Haworth, Esq. J.P.	Charles Heaton, Esq.	Robert Bolton, Esq.
James Barlow, Esq. J.P.	Thos. T. Pearson, Esq.	James Lever, Esq.
Joseph Musgrave, Esq. J.P.	William Boyes, Esq.	Dr. A. Cosgrave.

The Chair of the Evening Meeting will be occupied by

RICHARD HAWORTH, Esq., J.P., of Manchester.

Collections will be made in the Afternoon and Evening in behalf of the Building Fund.

A PROCESSION of Teachers, Scholars, and Friends, will start from the Institute at 3-45 p.m., headed by the Bradshaw Brass Band, under the conductorship of Mr. A. MONKS, of Stalybridge.

Notice publicising the corner-stone laying by Thomas Hardcastle.

pupils. James Lever of Harwood Lodge, West Scowcroft of Asmus and Samuel met the trustees of Walsh's Institute at Bank Street Chapel, Bolton to ask permission for the use of the Institute during the building of the new school; this was granted at a rent of £1 per month. The plans of the architects, Sherwood and Peverley of Manchester for the new school were accepted at a cost of £1250 and the land was given by Mr Thomas Hardcastle free from ground rent. The land was carefully marked out and measured on the corner of Longsight and Longsight Lane, 40 x 35 yards.

Many tenders for the building of the school were received and Mr Holt of Manchester got the contract for £1665, this was more than was expected but with a little negotiation it was reduced to £1600. On 1st May 1880 the scholars from the old school were moved to Walsh's Institute and on 3rd May the old school was demolished. Samuel watched as his old school disappeared into a pile of rubble.

The new Harwood Wesleyan School

The corner stone of the new school was laid by Mr Thomas Hardcastle of Bradshaw Hall on 26th June. Mrs Joseph Tootill presented him with a trowel and Samuel's wife gave him a mallet inscribed with the words: -

Presented to Thomas Hardcastle Esq. of Bradshaw Hall
by Mrs Samuel Scowcroft of Bradshaw,
in commemoration of his laying the corner stone of
the Harwood Wesleyan School, near Bolton.
JUNE 26TH 1880

A bottle time capsule was prepared by Samuel, Edwin and Abel Scowcroft, containing new coins, plans of the Wesley circuit for the current quarter, Methodist papers, copies of the Bolton Chronicle, Journal and Guardian, a photograph of the old school, a likeness of grandfather John Scowcroft and 20-30 other items; quite a collection. This container was placed under the cornerstone, where it was found in 1958 when the school was demolished. A tea party followed the laying of the stone, organised by the ladies, Mrs Joseph Tootill, Mrs John Scowcroft, Mrs Samuel Scowcroft, Mrs Richard Brown, Mrs James Bromiley, Mrs Matthew Holt and Mrs John Southern. Mr Richard Howarth, merchant of Manchester acted as chairman, while many other notable gentlemen were present at the party in Walsh's Institute.

Samuel was also on the Bradshaw School attendance committee; fitting in all the meetings must have been quite a formidable task and he relied on having a capable wife and assistant to look after the shop. Bradshaw new school was

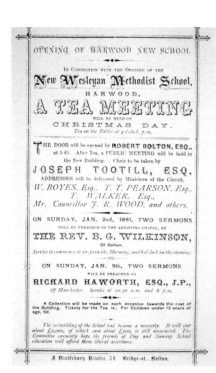

OPENING OF HARWOOD NEW SCHOOL

In Connection with the Opening of the

New Wesleyan Methodist School,

HARWOOD,

A TEA MEETING

WILL BE HELD ON

CHRISTMAS DAY.

Tea on the Tables at 4 o'clock, p.m.

THE DOOR will be opened by **ROBERT BOLTON, ESQ.,** at 3-45. After Tea, a PUBLIC MEETING will be held in the New Building. Chair to be taken by

JOSEPH TOOTILL, ESQ.

ADDRESSES will be delivered by Ministers of the Circuit,

W. BOYES, Esq., T. T. PEARSON, Esq., T. WALKER, Esq.,

Mr. Councillor *J. R. WOOD*, and others.

ON SUNDAY, JAN. 2nd, 1881, TWO SERMONS

WILL BE PREACHED IN THE ADJOINING CHAPEL, BY

THE REV. B. G. WILKINSON,

Of Bolton.

Service to commence at 10-30 in the Morning, and 6 o'clock in the evening.

ON SUNDAY, JAN. 9th, TWO SERMONS

WILL BE PREACHED BY

RICHARD HAWORTH, ESQ., J.P.,

Of Manchester. *Service at 10-30 a.m. and 6 p.m.*

A Collection will be made on each occasion towards the cost of the Building. Tickets for the Tea, 1s.; For Children under 13 years of age, 6d.

The re-building of the School had become a necessity. It will cost about £2,000, of which sum about £500, is still unsecured. The Committee earnestly hope the friends of Day and Sunday School education will afford them liberal assistance.

J. Bradbury, Printer, 54 Bridge-st., Bolton.

Notice of celebration on the opening of the New Wesleyan Methodist School January 1881.

The new Harwood Wesleyan School opened 1880.

*The Opening Ceremony at the new Bradshaw school on 21st August 1880
opened by the Lord of the Manor of Bradshaw, John Bradshaw Isherwood,
followed by tea at the pavilion.*

St Maxentius School, built at the junction of Bradshaw Chapel.

The Rev P.A.Galindo,
Vicar of Bradshaw who died on
the day the new
St. Maxentius School was
opened. 21st August 1880.

now ready for the opening ceremony on 21st August 1880 but unfortunately Reverend P.A.Galindo the Vicar of Bradshaw Church died on the morning of the opening. The new school was opened by Mr John Bradshaw Isherwood of Marple Hall, Cheshire who was presented with the key by Mrs Richard Wild; a tea party followed in the Pavilion.

Later there was a meeting in the old school regarding adoption of the new byelaws, which was adjourned, but at a later meeting in the new school, the committee agreed to put them into effect. The byelaws in this case would follow from the recent Education Act, which stated that children should compulsorily attend school until they reached the age of 10.

Samuel spent his time shuttling between Bradshaw School and Harwood Wesleyan School and in December 1880 the new heating system for the Wesleyan School was completed and ready for testing. Samuel with other members of the committee helped to fill the water tank and light the fire, all appeared to be working. Everything was now ready including closets, or toilets as they now called, and the new school was ready for the opening ceremony at Christmas 1880. Samuel's cousin, Robert Bolton, was presented with a silver key by Mrs James Bromiley to open the door of the school. Tea was provided at the meeting held afterwards with many speeches given by Reverend Marshall Randles (superintendent minister), Joseph Tootill, Mr Boyce of Bolton, Richard

Lee, brother John and several others. This school remained in use until 1958 when a new one was built in Longsight Lane which was subsequently demolished in 1985, the last Methodist school in Harwood. The site is now occupied by houses.

There had been various rumours for quite a while that a water supply was being piped to Bradshaw and the local property owners called a meeting with the Sanitary Authority at Walsh's Institute to discuss the matter. The Sanitary Authority had inspected the local water supply in 1880 and found that a number of wells and water cisterns in the area were only suitable for washing, or cattle and not for personal drinking. At a meeting in July 1881 it was proposed by Thomas Hardcastle and seconded by Robert Booth that the local water supply was sufficient and of quite good quality and Bolton Corporation water was declined for the present.

After all the harassment of these meetings, Samuel needed a day off to relax, so to get away from it all he went with friends for a day's shooting at Marsh Farm, Thornton. He was pleased with the results – 1 hare, 1 rabbit and 4 seagulls. No animal rights groups in those days but one wonders if they had seagull pie. Then it was home to Bradshaw and back to everyday happenings.

The next requirement on the agenda was to equip Harwood Wesleyan School. Samuel went with Joseph Tootill to Manchester to purchase items of furniture including 12 writing desks, 60 yards of plain forms, 23 yards of forms with backs, a master's desk, sewing table, 2 desks for classrooms, 3 blackboards, maps, inkwells and several sundries.

Samuel wasn't immune to accidents - on a trip to Bolton he was thrown out of his cart when his pony slipped on the Welsh setts, however as he wasn't going at a fast trot he was only slightly hurt. He probably wasn't concentrating on guiding his pony carefully in the slippery conditions, his mind being full of other affairs.

Gas Lamps

Exciting times arrived when gas was piped to light Bolton Road in March 1882. Gas lamps were erected between Bradshaw Bridge and Bradshaw Smithy on Lee Gate and the road became well lit and safer in the dark. The lampposts to Bradshaw Hall and to Harwood followed later. Also in March at the Harwood Township meeting, Samuel's brother John was re-elected as Guardian and Joseph Tootill as surveyor. At the Bradshaw Township meeting, John Priestley and Thomas Hardcastle were re-elected Guardians and Joseph Greenhalgh and

Samuel as overseers. Samuel was delighted with the result of this election and was later re-elected in 1885.

Duty of Overseer

The overseers for Bradshaw and later Harwood were responsible for collecting rates and administering relief to the poor. This consisted of very small amounts to help with rent and feeding the family before they became destitute and had to go to the workhouse. Fortunately for Samuel, he was wealthy by comparison and was able to buy property. About this time he purchased seven cottages and land that came up for sale on Cox Green Road, near the Flag Inn.

Samuel's son, Samuel Jnr., now 15 and attending Bolton Church Institute School was a very intelligent boy. His father was very proud and his delight knew no bounds when Samuel was presented with a book prize at the Albert Hall, Bolton by the Dean of Chester. Samuel never boasted about his children but was privately happy with their success at school.

In February 1884 after a previous committee meeting, Samuel went with Mr Alfred Booth, the headmaster of Harwood Wesleyan School to Cheadle to look at a billiard table for Walsh's Institute. After consultation with the trustees, a decision was made to purchase the table at a cost of £40. In the same month the bill arrived for the new school from Sherwood and Peverley the architects, the total cost was £2,100, including £1,735 for the builders. There had been an increase on the original price of £42 10 shillings for heating, £88 10 shillings for walls, fences and closets and £3 10 shillings for plastering the inside walls.

When Samuel's mother was 84 on 22nd November 1883 he commissioned David Winder to paint her portrait in oils; this was completed in February 1884 and exhibited at the art gallery exhibition in Bolton Mechanics Institute. Until a few years ago there was an art shop in Great Moor Street under the name of Winders.

On 9th April 1884, brother John was once again re-elected Guardian for Harwood after the counting of the voting papers at the Mawdsley Street Poor Law Office. He remained Guardian for seven years. On the same day Harwood Wesleyan Bazaar was opened by Thomas Hardcastle of Bradshaw Hall, this was a five-day event, which raised £704, much more than was expected; the amount after deduction of expenses was £669. Samuel's contribution to this affair was to write letters asking for gifts. One reply was from Sir Stafford Northcote who sent eleven autographed photographs of himself to be sold at the bazaar.

1881

March 2 { Sarah } The wife of Peter Haslam (Meadow Barn farm) died this forenoon

" 2 Fire at Nathan Ramsden's croft. Brooks Bank Harwood. This is the second fire there within 18 months

" 5 Buried Sarah Haslam of Meadow Barn at Bradshaw Ch.

" 13 Emperor Alexander of Russia. Killed by a Bomb.

" 24 Jethro Crossley (Tho⁵ Son) died   Buried 27th at Bradshaw Ch.

" 25   Brown (Rich⁴ daughter) died   28th Buried at Harwood Meth Chape

" 26 John Greenhalgh (Black Cock) died   Buried on the 30th

" 27 Tho⁵ Bridge (Bradshaw Chapel) house on fire slight damage done

" 28 Another fall of snow during last night. The hills round here Edgworth & Holcombe not having been clear of snow for 12 weeks.

" 29 Wm Keble Bradshaw Brow died this morning

30 Turton Local Board Election for South Ward two members to be elected Sam¹ Kay (farmer) 254. James Fletcher 296 Turton Lane. Sam¹ Brooks 139 Leygate Harwood. James Bromiley 115 B Brow. votes

April 1 John Walmsley old died at Nanny Pollitts house side of Smithy.

" 4th For Census of England & Wales (made up by me as follows for our House)

1 Sam¹ Scowcroft	Head of family	Married	42	Grocer Draper & Corn dealer	Lancashire	Bradshaw Chapel
2 Elizabeth Do	Wife	Married	40	Do	Do	Wife	Do	Turton
3 Edith Do	Daughter		15	"	"	Daughter	Do	B Chapel
4 Sam¹ Do	Son	U	12	"	"	Son	Do	Do
5 Peter Alfred Do	Son	U	7	"	"	Son	Do	Do
6 Rob¹ Bolton Do	Son	U	3	"	"	Son	Do	Do
7 Jane Scowcroft	Mother	Widow	81				Do	Harwood Meth Bolton
8 Harriet Plant	Servant	Unmarried	18	General servant	Shropshire	Ch Ashton

Diary entry for 1881 showing Samuel Scowcroft's entry for his family in the 1881 Census Return.

THE FOLLOWING

SHOPKEEPERS

CLOSE

THEIR

SHOPS

AT

SEVEN O'CLOCK ON SATURDAYS,

AND

Half-past Seven on other Week Nights.

Trusting our Customers will support us in the above movement,

We remain,

Yours.

SAMUEL SCOWCROWT, JUNR.

A. & E. UNSWORTH.

JAS. BROMILEY.

JAN. 1ST, 1879.

The EVENING NEWS and JOURNAL Offices, Infirmary-st., Bolton.

An 1879 notice showing the local shop closing times.

The Workhouse built by the Bolton Union at Fishpool,
a district of Farnworth, in 1861.

Mains Water to Bradshaw and Harwood

The problem of water was once again raised when, after 3 years from the first approach by Bolton, the property owners had to concede defeat to the Corporation and accept their water supply to the Hardcastle houses on Lee Gate Lane and to Samuel's on Bradshaw Road. The conclusion of the Sanitary Authority was that the well water was not fit to drink. The water main was continued to Nab Gate and, via the White Horse, to Bottom o'th'Moor by June 1884.

A Visit to Scotland

Samuel needed a holiday to relax, away from the hassle with the water authority; he knew the shop would be well looked after by his wife and son Samuel. In July he decided he would like to visit Scotland, as he had never been there before, so Samuel with his friend Joseph Tootill set off on Saturday by train to Edinburgh. After a seven-hour journey they arrived and stayed at the Waverley Hotel but they weren't too exhausted to go to a concert given by soldiers in the evening. On the next day, Sunday, they attended a service at St Giles Church. The holiday really started on Monday when Samuel and Joseph went from Edinburgh to Oban via Glasgow, Greenock, Kyles of Bute and the Crinan Canal, staying at the Argyle Hotel. On Tuesday they left Oban by rail for Crianlarich station, took a coach to Loch Lomond and a steamer to Roardennan Hotel. Before bedtime they took a 2-3 mile walk up Ben Lomond. On Wednesday they went from Loch Lomond by coach to Loch Katrine, took a boat down the loch, another coach through the Trossachs to Callender and then took the train to Stirling. Still full of energy they visited the castle and cemetery and walked to the monument. On Thursday they left Stirling for home via Glasgow, Carlisle, Preston and Bolton, having been away six days. Samuel had enjoyed the delights of sailing and the sights of the mountains, glens, lochs and canals; quite an awe inspiring holiday which fired his blood for future visits.

Samuel, as overseer for Bradshaw, had several days away from home in September 1884, when he went with other dignitaries from Bolton to Wigan to see Mr Gladstone, the prime minister and his wife, whose train had stopped for a short while on it's return journey from Scotland. Mr Gladstone was welcomed and a few speeches made; Samuel shook hands with Mrs Gladstone but before he could shake hands with Mr Gladstone the train had to leave the station.

In December of the same year at a meeting of the Harwood Wesleyan School Samuel was elected onto the Day School managers committee along with eight other members. It appears that Samuel had his feet in both camps, as he was already a member of the Bradshaw School Managers Board.

1884   48

Aug 27 James Greenhalgh (Twin Keck) died at Longsight aged 54

„ 30   John Haydock (Sam'son) And Miss Gardiner married at Brad Ch

Sep 23 Epidemic of Measels Bradshaw & neighbourhood Thos. Henry Slater child died

„ 24   „   „ Wm Henry Rostron child died effects of Measles

„ 25   „ Thos Shaw child died   Do

„ 26   Went to Wigan saw Wm E Gladstone shook hands with Mrs Gladstone

„   was going to do so with Mr G. the train got in motion and he motioned to

       me to keep away from the train. they were returning from Scotland

Oct 4   A man named Dugdale a commercial traveller found near

       the Ch Institute Bolton (off Bradshawgate) Murdered he was robbed of his

       money. Kay Howarth of Egerton taken into custody on suspicion.

Oct 17 Alice Whittle (Peter widow wife and Joe Mother) died at her daughter Jane's Buried on 20th B. Ch.

„ 18   James Hamer (Banker) fell down stairs in Brookfold lane

„ 19   Edward Ormrods' wife died in Leegate

„ 20   Alice Scholes (Wm wife) died affitside lane

„ 26   James Holt (John Banns son) and Mary Storey married

Nov 1   Wm Ramwell (Thos Son) and Miss Brooks — Joseph Heywood (Jonh Son)

       And Alice Bromily (Ralph daughter)   Ellis Waring (Arch Son) and Miss

       Booth married married at Bradshaw Ch

Nov 4   Kay Howarth sentenced to be hung for the Murder of R Dugdale

Nov 10 Peter Roscow (Peter Son) died at Bradshaw Brow

„ 12   Charlotte Ramsden (Johns wife) died opposite the Ship Brad Chapel
       in the room I was born in.   She was Buried at Brad ch 16th

*Diary entries Aug to Nov 1884, including Samuel's visit to see
Mr & Mrs Gladstone at Wigan Station.*

Samuel's brother Richard, who had a shop and post office in Bradshaw Road, also opened a money order service and Post Office Savings Bank in September 1885; this was intended to encourage people to save money for holidays, retirement and rainy days. One can't imagine that there would be much money remaining at the end of the week to save. Even in those days of low wages there would be the savers and spenders.

Samuel had a disappointment in April 1886 when his very reliable and capable assistant Abel Scowcroft decided to leave the shop and go to work on his own account at James Bromley's shop, Bradshaw Brow. Fortunately for Samuel, his son Samuel, now 18 was able to run the business alongside his mother. Samuel senior would still be able to perform his other village duties and have regular holidays.

On retirement from office in 1886, one had to rely on the goodwill of various committees for a suitable pension, an example of this was at the Overseers Committee meeting in August when they recommended to the Local Guardian Board that on the retirement of John Wood, rate collector, he should be awarded £50 a year superannuation. A comfortable sum for that period which, with any savings he had in the Post Office, would save him from the threat of ending his days in the workhouse. Samuel, who was on the committee didn't vote for this, as he wasn't in full agreement!

A sad day occurred for brother Richard on August 7th 1886 when his second wife Catherine died and was buried at Harwood Church. Richard and Catherine had been married 25 years and had a son named Frederick. On 22nd August 1886, Frederick married Harriet Plant at Edgworth Wesleyan Chapel; she had been the servant to Samuel's family. Catherine didn't live long enough to see her son married, which must have been a sad day for everyone. After the marriage of Harriet to Frederick, Samuel's mother was becoming weaker, so it was necessary to employ another servant. In September Samuel employed Jane Clarke to take care of his family and his ageing mother. Jane later married Peter Haslam of Spring Side Farm, Harwood. On 22nd November Samuel's mother was 87 years old and had become very weak but was still able to have all her family with her for a little celebration. In Samuel's diary there were no recordings of any family parties to celebrate births, marriages, or even birthdays. Perhaps he organised enough concerts and celebrations at the chapel to feel it wasn't necessary for further entertainments.

Queen Victoria's Golden Jubilee

Early in 1887, the year of Queen Victoria's Golden Jubilee, a most important decision had to be made on a suitable celebration. A meeting was called at

Bradshaw School where it was decided that 4 representatives from Bradshaw Church, 4 from Harwood Wesleyan Church (of which Samuel was a member) and 4 from Harwood Primitive Methodist Church, would form a committee calling themselves 'The Jubilee Celebration Committee'. Thomas Hardcastle and J.T.S. Garnett, two influential employers, were invited to the next meeting at which the date chosen for the celebration was 20th June 1887. A procession would be formed by the three churches, tea would follow in the individual schools and a charge of 4d for adults and 2d for children under 13 would be made. The procession would be accompanied by Bradshaw Brass and Fife Bands, after which it would disperse for tea, then form again to be led to Adam Field, Bradshaw, for sports. A large number attended, it was a complete success and a wonderful day. In the year 2002, for our Queen Elizabeth's Golden Jubilee, we celebrated with fireworks, pop concerts and other extravaganza.

Bradshaw had it's own quiet celebrations when in August 1887 a decision was made that the houses in Bradshaw Chapel and Lee Gate should be numbered. With there being only a small group of houses it wasn't previously thought to be essential but to start with No 74 seems very unusual!

Samuel attended the funeral of James Barlow of Greenthorne, Edgworth at the Edgworth Wesleyan Chapel in August 1887. There were 70 carriages and thousands of people lining the road from his home to the chapel. He was a very well respected and notable figure in the area. In early 1888 Samuel's mother, now 87 years old, was becoming weaker and bedridden. Samuel, for light entertainment and to get away from sickness and death, took himself to Buffalo Bill's Wild West show in Manchester; he was much more relaxed by the time he returned home - this kind of entertainment didn't seem to fit in with his usual lifestyle. A few weeks later as a treat for his wife Lizzie, he took her to Barrow-in-Furness for a day where they walked up to the cemetery for a view of the Isle of Man; the following week they went to hear Madam Albino sing at Blackpool's Winter Gardens and visited relatives in St Annes. Samuel liked to do as much as possible in a day, this time he didn't fit in sailing, but it must have been exhausting for Lizzie trying to keep up with him.

Business was flourishing, so an extension to the new shop was necessary and in September 1888 Samuel started to build a storeroom at the end of the new shop nearest the church. During the construction of this extension, one of Mr Hartley's cows escaped, crashed through the drapery shop window and ruined a number of hats. Samuel's wife Lizzie was not amused as this was her domain.

*Samuel Scowcroft's shop, No 1 Turton Road on Bradshaw Brow.
The children appear to be awaiting a procession. c.1910.*

*A view of Bradshaw Chapel, showing Samuels 'new shop' to the right (built in
1871). Note the hats in the drapery section and
brother Richard's shop to the left, 1937.*

Harwood Wesleyan Church on a Sermons Day c.1900.

*Samuel and Elizabeth
Scowcroft c.1900.*

Manchester Ship Canal

Samuel still liked to visit other areas to see any important happenings and in December 1888 he visited his friends in Eccles to see the Manchester Ship Canal under construction. He was quite impressed with all the work involved in the making of the canal and to think that soon steam ships would sail from Liverpool to Manchester carrying goods to the centre of industrial Lancashire as well as returning with cargoes for all over the world. Queen Victoria officially opened the canal on 21st May 1894 although it was already in use by this date.

There was a sad day in January 1889 when Samuel's mother died at the age of 89 at Bradshaw Chapel. She was buried in Bradshaw Church yard by the Reverend R.K.Judson. Samuel's mother had been ill for a number of years and had become very forgetful; she was bedfast and had not eaten solid food for two years. In June Samuel again needed a relaxing break from the stress of everyday life. He arranged with his friends William Bridge, John Holt and Edwin Scowcroft to go to Windermere for two days. They visited Grasmere, walked to Keswick, stayed the night and returned by coach to Grasmere passing the Thirlmere water works which, when completed, was to supply water to Manchester. The friends stopped at various hostelries for bread, cheese and milk but not too often as they were stunned by what they saw as exorbitant prices. After the death of their mother, Richard and Samuel, as executors to their father's will, had to settle the affairs of Samuel senior when many properties had to be sold. There were six houses in Apple Street, Bolton and four houses in Leegate, the houses in Leegate being conveyed to William Laithwaite their brother-in-law. After the sale of everything, the proceeds were shared between the family, consisting of John, Sophia, Richard, Sarah Ann and Samuel, who, being astute business people invested the money in more property. John bought houses at Ruins, Harwood, Samuel bought four houses at Bradshaw Brow and sister Sophia purchased houses in Walkden. Samuel also extended his shop on Bradshaw Road at the end nearest Rigby Lane, brick pillars being erected for a corrugated iron shed.

Crimes of murder, rape, assault and robbery haven't changed much since Victorian times but punishment is now more lenient. In November 1889 a girl named Nelly Pomfret was assaulted by James Bierns on her way home to Harry Fold from Samuel's shop, where she had bought 2oz of twist tobacco. Samuel had to go as witness to Manchester Assizes to swear under oath that the tobacco found in the young man's possession was similar to that which was sold in the shop to Nellie Pomfret. James Bierns was found guilty and sentenced to four months hard labour and fifteen strokes with the cat. Today in the 21st Century it would be very different.

Turton Tower Sale

Samuel liked to go to sales to see if he could pick up any bargains; at Turton Tower there was a sale of furniture from the estate of the late James Kay in September 1890. The furniture was auctioned and some of the prices astounded Samuel. A bedstead destined for Kensington Museum cost 340 guineas and another one 70 guineas. He also attended the second day's sale and took Lizzie his wife with him, they didn't appear to buy anything so it must have been curiosity or everything was too expensive.

At the next Bradshaw Township meeting in March 1891, Samuel and Samuel Haslam were once again elected as overseers with Thomas Hardcastle as surveyor. Samuel had to sign the Poor Rate Book which was 2s 8d in the pound for the year; at the time there was no highway rate.

In April 1891, No 76 Bradshaw Chapel became vacant so Samuel and family had their furniture moved in and went there to live. It was originally the house of Jethro Scowcroft.

In July at Harwood Wesleyan Chapel, Samuel's brother John, whose first wife Hannah had died in February, married Anne Broughton Knowles, who had nursed his wife during her long illness. John died nine years later after catching a cold. He was buried in the same grave as Hannah.

The first meeting of the local committee to consider the County Council grant met at Walsh's Institute on 23rd November 1891, present were Thomas Hardcastle, chairman, Rev Rees, Rev Judson, J.B.Tootill, Ashworth Ashworth, A Kirkman and Samuel; only Dr Cosgrave was absent. The outcome was a yearly grant of £127 8s 11d for Harwood Wesleyan School.

First Harwood Wesleyan Magazine

At a committee meeting of the Harwood Wesleyan Chapel it was decided to introduce a church magazine with Number 1 published in January 1892. Samuel who must have had a few minutes to spare volunteered to be secretary and held this post for a number of years. The magazine is still published but the style has changed to a modern computerised edition.

Samuel and his wife had an invitation to visit Hawarden Castle, the home of Mr Gladstone the Prime Minister. They had a pleasant day and met an American gentleman there who took then back to Chester in his carriage. Samuel, now a well known member of many committees, came into contact with mill owners and other prominent people which led to many invitations.

Engraving of Turton Tower in the Auction Notice of September 1890, for the Sale of the late James Kay's Estate.

The cover of the Sept 1893 copy of the Harwood Wesleyan Magazine, Samuel was the committee secretary.

45

In April 1893, Samuel still as an overseer of Bradshaw Township, went to Bolton Town Hall to be sworn in as assessor of taxes together with J.J.Bentley.

Samuel's business had now expanded to the extent that he began to publish a catalogue called 'The Scowcroft Messenger' that described the articles he dealt with; the business was eventually taken over by his sons, Samuel and Robert Bolton.

Samuel took his wife away for a few days holiday in the summer of 1893. They went to Llandudno with Mrs Roscoe and stayed in Llanberis. Feeling very fit Samuel and Lizzie climbed Snowdon whilst they were there and included many other strenuous walks. They all returned home via Betws-y–Coed after an invigorating holiday; Mrs Roscoe was delighted with her visit to Llanberis.

Once again the Sanitary Authority appeared on the scene and called a meeting at the Poor Law office in Bolton to discuss the sewage scheme for Bradshaw. Samuel, James Rostron, Henry Turner Scowcroft and William Russell a solicitor attended. They arranged to take a deputation from the Rural Sanitary Authority around Bradshaw and Harwood to prove there was no pollution in the drinking water.

After this head to head confrontation with the Sanitary Authority Samuel was feeling a little work weary; he was now 55 and needed a rest. He took Lizzie on the train to Blackpool for a few days where the sea breezes soon dispersed his lethargy. Wherever Samuel went a sail was essential, so off to Fleetwood they went to catch a steamer to Morecambe, then via Lancaster to Barrow-in-Furness where they stayed with friends, the Edward Tootills. The next day they went off again to the Isle of Man on the Manx Queen where they stayed the night to recuperate; and the next day sailed back to Fleetwood. Their next stop was Blackpool, then Southport to call on their cousin Joseph Tootill. They visited the Hydro to see William Bridge, a painter from Bradshaw Brow who was being treated for injuries received in a railway accident at Horwich. Full of renewed energy Samuel and Lizzie then returned home to Bradshaw. The following year Samuel and Lizzie chose to go to Llanberis again as they had previously enjoyed climbing Snowdon and walking in the hills.

Guardian of Bradshaw

Back to the affairs of Bradshaw, in September 1894 Bradshaw Conservative Club asked Samuel to accept the office of Guardian for Bradshaw Township on Bolton Rural District Council. The office included responsibility for roads, and sanitation etc. Samuel was nominated by Thomas Hardcastle and accepted the proposal on the understanding that he attended when his time allowed, bearing in mind his other commitments.

On 5th December 1894 he was finally elected and a few weeks later attended his first meeting of the B.R.D.C Board of Guardians. The Rural Council comprised seventeen townships which had no previous local boards. A few months later Samuel went with the Rural District Council to inspect the highways of Edgworth, Harwood, Quarlton, Bradshaw and Breightmet prior to them being taken over by the T.U.D.C council in April 1895.

Sewage System

Since the mains water was laid in 1884, pressure came from the Sanitary Authority for a local sewage scheme. Samuel and the other overseers in Bradshaw and Harwood were determined to oppose this proposal and engaged the services of Mr John Lomax, surveyor of Bolton and Mr Herbert Hall solicitor of Bolton to represent them. Two days later in May 1895, the committee went with the surveyor to inspect the sewers and outlets into Bradshaw Brook. To prove their point Samuel caught two trout in the Ruins Brook near the gutter outlet. The following day the committee took the trout to the Local Government enquiry held at the Poor Law Office to prove there was no pollution in the brook. Samuel was examined by Mr H.Hall; the inspector took the evidence for further discussion and Bradshaw and Harwood had to await results. It was some years later in August 1897 before Samuel and the other property owners would bow down before the might of the Bolton Sanitary Authority and allow a sewage system to be connected from Bradshaw Bridge to Brookfold Lane, Harwood, the expenses being covered by Bradshaw and Harwood townships.

Marriage of daughter Edith

Another wonderful day was spent on 29th May 1895 when Samuel's much loved and only daughter Edith was married to Mr Arthur Adshead at Harwood Wesleyan Chapel by Rev. Barlow Brown. One can imagine that Samuel did a thorough search to make sure Arthur was suitable for his lovely daughter. A week after Edith's wedding, Samuel organised a holiday in Scotland with his nephew Edwin Scowcroft, staying the first night at the Waverley Hotel, Edinburgh. On the last visit Samuel had enjoyed himself so much he was determined to repeat his tour including as many sailing trips as possible. They travelled by coach and boat between Edinburgh and Oban where they met two of their relatives, Joseph and Jim Tootill. Next day they took a boat and then had an exhilarating coach ride over the mountains to Aberfoyle, before going on to Stirling by train. A visit to Stirling Castle was on the agenda, as Samuel never missed a visit there; he thought it was magnificent. After six days of mountains and lochs Samuel and Edwin returned home ready for any problems that came their way.

Samuel was beginning to relax thinking his business was doing well, when in November there was a fire in the room above the drapery store; it looked impossible to extinguish but Samuel, never one to panic, organised his neighbours, including Rev. Judson, and had the fire under control. Samuel was greatly relieved at saving the remainder of his business and, being an astute businessman, his shop was well insured and the claim quickly settled.

Visit to Port Sunlight

As a result of the many meetings that Samuel attended he had acquired several friends. One of these was James Lever, soap manufacturer of Harwood Lodge, whose son William had set up a new factory in Port Sunlight and built a model village for his workforce. On the death of his wife, James went to live with his son. James was very proud of the new factory and invited Samuel and Lizzie, to visit him and make a tour of the works. They duly admired all the departments of the soap factory then went to tea at his home 'Thornton Manor'. Samuel and Lizzie met the family they hadn't seen for a number of years and later were taken round the splendid village of Port Sunlight. They then saw the cricket and recreation ground which had been given by William for the villagers. William later became Lord Leverhulme in 1917. James Lever drove Samuel and Lizzie in his coach to the station where he presented Lizzie with a portrait of himself in remembrance of a lovely day.

Thornton Manor and contents, home of the Lever family were auctioned in 2001 and some pieces of interest were purchased by Bolton museum; these included a silver spade, a vase and a painting of Leverhulme's friend Jonathon Simpson whose granddaughter gave the money for the purchases. The key to Hall i' th' Wood was a gift and on loan are keys and ceremonial gavels from various Bolton Churches, which are now on display at the Hall i'th'Wood Museum.

With the increase in the local population, Harwood Wesleyan Chapel burial ground had become full and Samuel, as trustee, was asked to negotiate with Robert Bolton, his cousin, to buy some land. Robert Bolton agreed to give an acre of land near the church and this very generous offer was gratefully accepted by the Trustees in June 1897.

Queen Victoria's Diamond Jubilee

Queen Victoria's Diamond Jubilee was now approaching and a large procession was organised. Harwood Primitive Methodists, Harwood Wesleyan and

Bradshaw Church met at Bradshaw Chapel and walked via Turton Lane, Bradshaw Hall and Lee Gate, tea being provided in their own schoolrooms. Afterwards the three groups reassembled and proceeded to Adam Field for sports; later in the evening a large bonfire was lit by Mr Thomas Hardcastle. The day was organised by Mr T. Hardcastle as president, Joseph Whittle as secretary, Samuel as treasurer and four representatives from each church. The event took place on 22nd June 1897; it was a complete success and everyone enjoyed a happy and glorious day.

Marriage of Samuel Junior

Samuel junior was now 29 and he decided it was time to marry; he had known Annie Bamford for a number of years and arranged to marry her in September at Crumpsall Park Wesleyan Chapel, Manchester. After the celebration Samuel and Annie went to Scotland for their honeymoon returning to live in Rigby Lane before eventually moving to Church Street, Harwood which was convenient for their Bradshaw Chapel store. Samuel's brother Richard, sub postmaster at the shop at Bradshaw Chapel retired when he was 72, so the post office was moved to Bradshaw Brow to be under the direction of John Jones. The Post Office has moved many times over the years and it is now on Lee Gate.

New Burial Ground

The piece of land given by Robert Bolton was finally conveyed to the Harwood Wesleyan Chapel for the new burial ground. The document was witnessed by Mr Thomas Walker, farmer of Great Lever and by Samuel. The new ground was now ready for use; the first interment being a young girl from Castle Hill, on 21st December 1898.

Last Meeting of the Bolton Rural District Council

At election time on the 17th September 1898, the first nominations for Turton Urban District Council were proposed by Samuel, namely Thomas Hardcastle, Henry Turner Scowcroft and William Pilling. They were all elected and served up to the time of their death, as there was no opposition in subsequent elections. The last meeting of the Bolton Rural District Council was held at the Poor Law Office, Mawdsley Street, Bolton on 28th September 1898, when the elected members from each district were present. Samuel was also present at the last meeting on the 29th at the Fever Hospital, Rumworth as a member of the Bolton Rural District Council Hospital Committee. Following these final meetings the townships of Bradshaw, Harwood, Quarlton, Entwistle, Edgworth, Longworth and Belmont were incorporated into Turton Urban District Council from 30th September 1898.

Part of the front of Harwood Lodge, where James Lever lived for a while.

Thornton Manor acquired by James Lever and his son William (later to become Lord Leverhulme), and visited by Samuel and Lizzie Scowcroft.

New Farnworth Hospital

On 1st March 1899 the new hospital at Fishpool, Farnworth was opened. Samuel, his wife and daughter Edith were invited as guests. As the overseer for Bradshaw he had to make decisions on whether some inhabitants of Bradshaw and Harwood were so destitute they had to be sent to the workhouse. One can't imagine such poverty today in 2005, with social benefits to cover rent and food.

Later in this same month at election time Samuel was proposed as the Guardian of Bradshaw Ward by Thomas Hardcastle and seconded by James Kay, the contest was between Samuel and Ashworth Ashworth. At the election on 27th March Samuel became Guardian for Bradshaw and Harwood as the two townships were now combined, the position being for one year. The following year Samuel was re-elected for a further 3 years and finally served until 1912 when he was in his 70s.

Samuel was extremely busy with his various meetings but he still kept a keen eye on his business. In May 1899 he extended further by renting the corner shop on Bradshaw Brow – No 1 Turton Lane. He opened for business two weeks later and employed Mr Fairclough. The following year when the store became prosperous he extended the lease for a further fourteen years. Samuel managed to organise a few visits between his business and meetings to keep his wife happy. He took Lizzie to Haddon Hall, Chatsworth and to the opening of the new Tramp Ward off Deansgate, Bolton on June 22nd 1899. Two days later they were invited by the chairman of the Board of Wardens, John Heywood, to an 'at home' at the 'Pike' Bolton.

Bradshaw gradually moved with the times and the first electric trams from Bolton came to the Royal Oak, Bradshaw on a trial trip on the 30th October 1899. The brave passengers were members of Bolton Town Council.

1900

At the start of the new year, under 16 year olds were allowed alcoholic drinks. Samuel, being a keen member of the Temperance Society, went to a meeting of the Bolton Board of Guardians on 28th February 1900 where a resolution was passed in favour of a bill to stop the sale of intoxicants to persons under 16.

Samuel was also involved with acquiring an extra piece of land for Harwood Wesleyan School. In August he went to view the land with Mr Thomas Hardcastle, who had promised it to the school. It measured 25 yards from the school towards the Hillock, Bradshaw, 65 yards from the corner of Longsight Lane and 100 yards across the brickfield to the fence. The manse now stands on

One of the first electric trams to run from Bolton to the Bradshaw Brow terminus at the Royal Oak c.1900.

The new Bradshaw police station. Law and order was emphasised in Bradshaw when the County Police Station was built on Bolton Road opposite St Maxentius Church. The first stone was laid on 24th April 1900.

part of this land along with the Church Hall, the Scout Hut, Tennis courts and a car park.

Scotland

For the summer holiday of 1900 Samuel took Lizzie to Scotland for 10 days to show her the grandeur of the mountains and the wonders of the lochs and canals. They travelled by train to Edinburgh staying at the Old Waverley Hotel, Princess Street. The next day they toured Edinburgh and saw the castle and other famous buildings. A few days later they set off on Samuel's favourite journey, across to Dunoon. The following day they went to Oban and next day to Fort William, alighting from the boat at Ballachulish where they walked by Loch Leven to stretch their legs, and then caught the next boat to Fort William before returning to Oban. Whenever Samuel set foot in Scotland there was no stopping him and after a night at the Argyle Hotel they were off again by coach, train and steamer to Port Sonacan, then a 9 mile drive to Blairgowrie Falls before returning to Oban. Samuel organised as many steamers, train and coach journeys as he could fit into one day on the way to Stirling, where they stayed at the Royal Hotel. Next day, with coat tails flying they set off for Stirling Castle, the church, the cemetery and the Wallace monument all in one short morning. At twelve thirty they caught the train for Edinburgh and returned home to Bradshaw. Samuel was a very sprightly 62 and Lizzie 59, obviously they were not even out of breath and had both enjoyed a wonderful exhilarating holiday.

The Scowcrofts appeared to live to a ripe old age but it was still a sad time when one of them died. In October 1900 at the age of 82, Samuel's brother John died at home in Longsight opposite the school; he was buried at Harwood Wesleyan Chapel with his second wife Hannah.

Samuel knew his sons Samuel and Peter Alfred were capable of looking after the business but he still liked to keep his finger on the pulse. On taking stock of his horses and carts he came to the conclusion that he needed a fresh horse. He looked around the farm sales and auction markets until he saw a large black horse 17.2 hands high that was exactly what he required to pull his cart. The six years old horse cost £45, the family named him Jack; a year later their faithful pony Polly had to be destroyed.

Samuel had to switch his thoughts back from his business to guardianship affairs in November 1900 when the death of Walter Whitehead created a vacancy on the Assessment Committee of the Guardians. Samuel was proposed and elected without any opposition.

1901

In May 1901 Samuel had once again to cope with a death in the family when his sister Sophia who was nearly 80 years old caught cold after a visit to Bolton. She became very ill and two weeks later died at her cottage on Longsight belonging to Walsh's Institute. She was buried at Harwood Church. These cottages were eventually demolished around 1970.

In the summer holidays of 1901 Samuel and Lizzie went off again to Scotland; they couldn't resist the call of the mountains, glens and lochs. They spent their ten days sailing, walking, sightseeing and visiting wonderful waterfalls. Oban was a very popular place where they met many old friends from Bradshaw. They sailed back to Glasgow but said in future they would leave the boat at Greenock because of the smell of the river. Before returning home they visited the Glasgow exhibition, then in the afternoon caught the train back to Bolton. Both Samuel and Lizzie declared it was the finest holiday they had ever experienced.

During the years that Samuel was in office as Guardian and member of the Turton Urban District Council, the committee visited many hospitals including Carlisle Asylum and Workhouse, Lancaster County Asylum, Winwick Asylum and Liverpool New Sanatorium. These were not particularly pleasant days out but they helped the committee to assess possible improvements that could be made at Fishpool Workhouse and hospital in Farnworth. Whilst visiting Carlisle they couldn't resist a visit to the castle, cathedral and a walk round the town. When visiting Delamere Forest to see the Liverpool New Asylum, Mrs Greg a member of the committee who lived at Sandy Bank in Sharples but had a business in Styal, invited them all to tea in her cottage. On another occasion she provided a picnic tea in Delamere Forest after visiting Styal Homes, Oversly, as well as her cottage in Styal. From Lancaster they visited Morecambe and Heysham – the committee made the most of their days out. On 25th September 1901 the new nurses' home was opened in Fishpool Workhouse, a start to improved conditions.

Death of Queen Victoria and Coronation of Edward VII

After the death of Queen Victoria on 22nd January 1901, her eldest son Edward was crowned on 27th June 1902, and Bradshaw organised a coronation celebration. This took the usual form of a procession of all three churches involving 1600 people. They walked round Bradshaw and Harwood, then had tea in their own schools with sports to follow on Adam Field. Fireworks and balloons were provided and a huge bonfire was lit by Thomas Hardcastle. All went well and it was a spectacular day. After all the expenses were paid there was still £11 remaining, so the Celebration Committee decided to give the old folk a tea party in Bradshaw School; approximately 250 people over 60 years of age were invited. They had tea, entertainment and speeches giving everyone a wonderful evening.

August holidays came round again and Samuel and Lizzie went off to Scotland for ten days. They took the train to Edinburgh, stayed at the Waverley Hotel and next day went to Blairgowrie via Stirling, Dunblane and Perth. At Blairgowrie they were surprised to see acres of raspberry plants with scores of women gathering the fruit. In the evening they drove to see the famous Beech Fence where the trees are trimmed to form a high hedge along the roadside; it was a superb sight the likes of which Samuel would have liked to have seen along Bradshaw Road. Next day they left Blairgowrie for Braemar on an exhilarating journey in a coach drawn by horses over the Grampian Mountains and down Devil's Elbow where debris from a crashed motorcar littered the road; fortunately the occupants were only slightly injured and a bicycle hung on a post to warn travellers of the danger. They arrived at the hotel in Braemar about 6pm. In the evening to stretch their legs after the 36-mile coach ride, they walked 3 miles to Mar Lodge, the Duke of Fife's estate to see the red deer. The next day they left Braemar for Ballater, another 18 mile coach ride along a fine road passing Balmoral Estate, the King's residence, arriving at Ballater station for the train to Aberdeen and then Inverness where they stayed at the Station Hotel. Following all this coach riding they sailed from Inverness down the Caledonian canal to Fort William. After a leisurely tea, Lizzie and Samuel walked to the foot of Ben Nevis, from there they went to Oban. The next day being Sunday they had a quiet day, going to church morning and evening.

By Monday they had renewed their energy so off they went again by boat to Tarbet to watch the fishing fleet leave the harbour. Early next morning they left by boat for Gourock, took a tram ride to view the town and returned by train to Edinburgh to catch the train to Bolton after a fantastic holiday with perfect weather. To organise this holiday with 7 hotels, trains, horse drawn coaches, steamers and trams was quite a feat; it was not surprising that Samuel was always in great demand as a committee member.

Death of Thomas Hardcastle

On 29th September 1902 Thomas Hardcastle died at Blaston Hall, his estate in Leicestershire and his body was brought back to Bradshaw Hall for a funeral service at Bradshaw Church. Samuel, Richard and Samuel junior received invitations to attend at the Hall and follow the funeral procession to the church on 2nd October 1902. A large crowd lined the road as a mark of respect to the memory of a man who had endeared himself in the hearts of many. A few days

John Scowcroft, Samuel's brother who died in 1900.

Edwin Scowcroft, John's son, who accompanied Samuel on many of his holiday trips.

Edwin Scowcroft 1843 – 1931, seen in his garden at 381 Church Lane (Stitch-mi-Lane). This terrace of three cottages was then known as 'Diamond Row'.

later the coffin was taken to Bromley Cross station for the journey back to Blaston Hall to be interred at nearby Horninghold.

Following the death of Thomas Hardcastle, Samuel and Mr W Holt had the task of visiting his son Henry Hardcastle to discuss land promised to Harwood Wesleyan School by his father. A plan of the land was inspected with the area marked out that had not yet been conveyed to the trustees of Harwood Wesleyan School. To keep everything friendly and making sure the conveyance would go forward smoothly, Samuel proposed and Richard seconded that Henry Marmaduke Hardcastle should fill the vacancy on the Turton Urban District Council left by the death of his father. He was returned unopposed.

The Scowcrofts were often called on to raise money for Harwood Wesleyan Chapel and School and organised a three days Conversazione at the school over Christmas 1902. The first day's events were opened by Samuel's granddaughter Evelyn Adshead and Herbert Holt. The second day by cousin John Scowcroft and Isaiah Dootson as chairman, the third day by Mrs J.B.Gass with Mrs Richard Lee as chairwoman. An excellent sum of £82.12s was raised and a few months later a Young Woman's Soiree raised a further £31.

Electric Trams

In March 1903 Samuel was invited to a reception at the Town Hall Square where three electric trams arrived direct from Liverpool with members of Liverpool Corporation. It was a very exciting moment to know that Bolton Tramways was now connected with Liverpool via The Lane Ends, Hulton. (Four Lane Ends, Overhulton).

In April, Harwood Wesleyan Chapel was renovated or beautified, in Samuel's words. The Mayor of Bolton, John Miles, presided at the reopening ceremony and played a selection of organ music. The actual re-opening was performed by Councillor and Guardian J.T.Brooks. In May the Edgworth and District Agricultural Society show was held at Bromley Cross. The Scowcrofts enjoyed the day out especially as Samuel junior, now aged 35, had a stallion on show; with his strong Scowcroft character he would no doubt be hoping to be presented with a prize. In later years Samuel's sons displayed cheeses at the show and won a first prize.

Inquests

Another duty performed from time to time by Samuel was foreman of the Jury on inquests, held at the Crofters Arms or Bulls Head Inn, concerning persons found drowned in the various local lodges.

Celebration Processions for King Edward VII Coronation, 27th June 1902.

S. MAXENTIUS', BRADSHAW.

NOVEMBER, 1902.

THOMAS HARDCASTLE,

DIED SATURDAY, SEPTEMBER 27th, 1902, aged 66.

Mr. Hardcastle had been in failing health for some little time, but the news of his death came as a great shock. The mind went back on his kindness and goodness, on the many kind, gracious things he had done among us for so many years. We were hoping that in God's good time, by His merciful loving over-rule, there would have been a happy working out of things, and a healing of the difference of the last few years. There were signs of this, and we were looking forward to his spending many years of peaceful, happy old age among us. God in His love has seen fit to order otherwise; but we are sure that all that is true, and good, and beautiful—all that is likest God in us is only purified and deepened by death; and though we see not those who have passed 'within the veil,' we can love them still, and they us—as never before; we can rejoice together in our Father's love, and the wondrous working of that love. We are reminded of Mr. Hardcastle's interest in everything connected with the parish at every turn—the Church—Mr. Galindo's failing health and the help he was to him—the great pavilion built for school and parish purposes—the new school—the site for the Vicarage—the Church Army Mission—his interest in the senior men's class—the treats to the children—and so much besides in connexion with church and school and out in the parish and elsewhere. God judges more kindly than we do; and they who are brought nearer Him see

"With larger, other eyes than ours."

Let us try to look at things as God sees them, and as he, who has gone out of our sight, sees them now. If here—in our wilful, stumbling lives—we want what is good and true, and to love one another, and to do our duty—how much more in that clearer light and purer atmosphere? We know what the love of the Father, of Jesus Christ the son of God, of the Holy Spirit, is looking for and working for—" A new commandment I give unto you, that ye also may love one another, as I have loved you." A new call to love and duty has come to us— a new look into the unseen, a new bond made between us here in the flesh, and those ' within the veil.'

We regret that Mr. Hardcastle was not buried at Bradshaw. His body was brought here from Blaston, where he died : and the funeral arranged for Thursday, October 2nd ; but a memorandum was found written in a broken hand, probably but a day or two before his death, that he wished to be buried quietly at Horninghold, close by Blaston. It had been publicly announced that the funeral would take place at Bradshaw. As this could not be, a memorial service was arranged for the Thursday, before the body was taken back to Blaston. The body was carried from the Hall to the Church by the foremen at the works, followed by a long procession of mourners—friends and senior scholars and representatives of public bodies. The Day School children joined in and walked as far as the church. Hundreds of people were about the church and churchyard shewing their sympathy. All the members of the choir who were able took part in the service, which was very impressive. The hymns sung were—" Now the labourer's task is o'er " ; and " There is a Green Hill far away." The body remained in Church all night. A light was kept burning, and the body was never left till it was removed to Blaston next morning. The burial took place at Horninghold, on Saturday, October 4th.

The report of Thomas Hardcastle's death and funeral in the
St Maxentius Parish Magazine, Nov 1902.

The Rigby Mission Hall built by Thomas Hardcastle from part of Rigby's Bleachworks.

A 1942 photograph taken at the Rigby's 50yrs celebration. The tablet to the memory of Thomas Hardcastle is in the right rear. On the back row next to the T.U.D.C. Chairman are Colonel Hardcastle, George Ashworth, Arthur Ashworth, the local clergyman and ladies.

The Rigby's Men's Bible Class ready for a 'trip'. The solid tyred 'chara' is parked near the corner of Turton Road.

The Scowcroft family had quite a shock in July 1903 when Samuel's brother Richard died after only a week's illness. Richard had returned from a few days holiday in Fleetwood feeling very poorly and gradually becoming weaker. His family were very concerned and visited him until his death. He was buried at Harwood Church on 20th July 1903.

Samuel seems to have set a pattern of taking a long holiday in August and in 1903 Samuel and Lizzie took Annie Bridge with them, as she needed a holiday. They chose Scotland again, their favourite haunt. They enjoyed twelve days full of sightseeing, went to church, sailed on the lochs, walked in the glens and all returned home refreshed. Samuel always enjoyed a day's shooting, not then thought suitable for a woman, so he would take his wife Lizzie to St Annes to visit their daughter Edith whilst he went off with his friends, mainly to the Kirkham area where they would shoot partridge and hares. In the evening he would travel back to St Annes to join his family, all well organised and everyone happy.

Samuel went to the unveiling on 26th September 1903 of a tablet at the Rigby Mission room by Colonel Ainsworth of Smithills in memory of Thomas Hardcastle who had built the three missions in the area, Riding Gate, Bradshaw Road and Rigby Mission.

New Toilets for Harwood Wesleyan Chapel

A very important meeting took place in late 1903 when Samuel went with Walter Holt as committee member for Harwood Wesleyan Chapel to see the builder Stanley Walker regarding closets in the chapel yard. A few days later the Rev A.Wells also went to see the existing closets or toilets at the entrance to the burial ground and the site where the new ones were likely to be built. We presume they came to an amicable decision, as there was no further mention of closets or toilets.

A new Education Act had come into force and a New Management Committee for Harwood Wesleyan School had to be formed. The old committee was disbanded and new members elected, one of whom was Samuel. The recent discussion regarding new toilets was related to the new act; even in 1903 they must have been concerned with health and hygiene.

Two and a half years after the death of Samuel's sister Sophia, her houses in Walkden went for auction at the Stocks Inn, Walkden. Samuel was there to keep an eye on the event and £500 was raised. A very useful sum in November 1903; no entry was made as to who received the money.

Nurse Pickles, the first Bradshaw District Nurse for whom Samuel gained a subscription from the Board of Guardians.

An early Bradshaw School group outside the newly built-in basement, c. 1905.

St Maxentius School Boy's playground c.1910. The built-in basement can be seen to rear.

Samuel must have had a very persuasive tongue, as at the Board of Guardians committee meeting he asked for a subscription for Bradshaw and District Nursing Committee and was unanimously granted the sum of £10.10s.0d, this was presented on December 30th 1903.

To celebrate Christmas 1903 a three-day 'Conversazione' was organised at Harwood Wesleyan School. On the first day the opener was Mr William Russell, solicitor of Bolton with Mr William Ward, cotton spinner of Bromley Cross as chairman. The second day was opened by Alice Booth with John Vickers as chairman, the third day by Edith Haslam and Mrs Leigh in the chair. The total raised was £55, not a great deal for all the hard work involved but the visitors would enjoy every moment.

Samuel's shop at 53 Tonge Moor Road was painted and decorated in January 1904 after which it was known as 'the white shop'. During this period James Lomax was the shop assistant.

Volunteers to Serve in South Africa

Samuel and Lizzie continued to have many invitations to ceremonial affairs in Bolton and they were invited by the mayor to a reception in the Town Hall in March 1904. This was held in the Albert Hall and was conducted by Colonel Gilbert John French who was unveiling a tablet and presenting prizes to the men who had served in South Africa. A few weeks later Colonel French once again called on Samuel to help recruit more volunteers for South Africa. Meetings were held in Walsh's Institute and Bradshaw School where sixteen young men joined the volunteer corps. In June 1907, Samuel and Lizzie were invited by Colonel French to the inspection of the volunteers in the Town Hall Square by General Fry and afterwards to a special meeting at the Temperance Hall.

New Classrooms at Bradshaw School

The number of pupils at Bradshaw School was increasing and there was a need for new classrooms. The management committee, of which Samuel was a member, decided that new classrooms should be organised in the basements of the school, these were completed on 10th April 1904.

Samuel, already on the Board of Guardians was also elected to the Finance Assessment and Workhouse Committee. By attending these various committees he was always in the eye of notable people who saw to it that he was invited to important occasions. In May 1904 when Rivington Park was given to Bolton Corporation by William Hesketh Lever, Samuel was invited to this grand affair when he was presented with a book by William Hesketh Lever.

Another exciting day was in June when Samuel had a telephone installed in his shop; the first person he called was Edith his favourite child who already had a telephone in her home on Turton Road. In 1904 there would be few people with telephones, other than business people, the wealthy and Scowcroft relations.

Means of travel weren't as sophisticated as today and when the Guardians organised a picnic to Bolton Abbey they went by train to Skipton and drove in brakes and wagonettes to the Abbey. It would have been quite a procession as there were 78 people in the party, carried in a convoy of different vehicles. The people who lived along the route would be outside their homes to watch in amazement. The following year the Guardians took their picnic to Windermere.

Two weeks later a deputation from the Turton Urban District Council went to London as the Bolton Corporation Water Bill was now before a committee of the House of Commons; Samuel and the other members were hoping to get the best possible terms for the district.

Samuel, being a member of the committee for the Bolton Workhouse, liked to keep in contact with other local activities and in August a sports day was organised to which he took his wife Lizzie and his granddaughter Evelyn. I don't think Samuel would have participated, as by then he was nearly 66. Following all this excitement, the next day he took Arthur his son-in-law, Edith, Evelyn and his wife Lizzie for a sail from Llandudno to Liverpool; he needed fresh sea breezes to renew his energies. This trip started him thinking of holidays again and he took Lizzie for a 12 days holiday to St Annes for sailing, walking and visiting friends and relations.

New Seats in Bradshaw

In November 1904 there was still money remaining after Queen Victoria's diamond jubilee celebration and Samuel proposed that eight seats be fixed on Bradshaw Road. Turton Council accepted with thanks and a promise to maintain them in the future. The cost of the seats was £10.12s.0d and they were finally in position by May 1905. After a number of fires in the Bradshaw Chapel locality Samuel came to the conclusion that a stand pipe and hose was necessary so he had one fitted into his shop ready for any emergencies, water was no longer a problem now there was a mains supply.

In January 1905 the land for Harwood Wesleyan school, promised by Thomas Hardcastle, had still not been conveyed to the trustees. Samuel notified Colonel Hardcastle and they fixed a meeting to see the land. Marker pegs were already in place so the Colonel promised to have the land conveyed immediately. He thought the land promised by his father was for a public playground so Samuel had to inform him that wasn't the case. The final deed was signed by Samuel as a trustee for Harwood Wesleyan School in July 1906. The acre of land given by Robert Bolton however was for a public playground being part of Posey Bank Farm and was promised in 1905 and conveyed in February 1906 to Turton Urban District Council.

Samuel junior decided to live nearer the shop and moved house from Rigby Lane to Church Street, Harwood. Samuel agreed to buy the house at 33 Longsight and transfer it to his son Peter Alfred who was about to marry Annie Farnworth on 24th April 1905 at Deane Church. It seemed possible that Samuel gave his son the house as a wedding present.

Holidays

Each year Samuel had to have sight of the sea, so off he went to St Annes for a few days with his wife, his daughter Edith, son-in-law Arthur and granddaughter Evelyn. They travelled from St Annes to Barrow-in Furness, Windermere, Coniston, Fleetwood, Blackpool and back to St Annes – what a fantastic tour at a cost of 7s 6d. Later in the year they all went to the Isle of Man for a few days, visiting all the towns there before returning to Heysham. The next journey was to Northern Ireland; there was no stopping Samuel when he went on his holidays. On arrival and after a short rest they went in tramcars drawn by horses on a tour of Belfast. The next day they went off to Portrush and Giant's Causeway which Samuel had visited forty years previously. The locals told stories of the giants who strode across the stepping-stones to Scotland, strangely only children saw the giants! Samuel, on his many visits to Northern Ireland went regularly to the causeway, a giant in himself if not in stature; maybe he was a secret believer. They spent ten days holiday in Ireland then travelled back to Bradshaw, but not before having a final look round Morecambe. Samuel was 67 the next day and the holiday certainly tested his stamina.

Ireland

Arthur, Samuel's son-in-law and a shipping agent, had started to work in Belfast in October 1905, so Arthur and Edith purchased a house in Knock about three miles from Belfast where they moved two weeks later from their house in Turton Lane. Samuel wasn't very happy at the thought of his favourite child being so far away. He waited two weeks before he took Lizzie over to see them and stayed for a week before returning, suffering a very rough sea passage. Three weeks later Arthur, Edith and Evelyn sailed from Belfast to Heysham then on to Bradshaw to spend Christmas at Bradshaw Chapel. Samuel was delighted as all his family sat down to their Christmas dinner together. Although Samuel had been worried that he wouldn't see his daughter

OLD BARN, LEVER PARK.

OPENING of

LEVER PARK, RIVINGTON,

By W. T. MASON, Esq.. M.A.

LUNCHEON AT 1·30 P.M.

MENU.

JULIEN SOUP.

MAYONNAISE OF SALMON.   PRAWNS IN ASPIC.

ROAST CHICKEN.   CHICKEN A LA BECHAMEL.
          YORK HAM.   OX TONGUE.
     ROAST LAMB.   SPICED BRISKET BEEF.
     POTATO SALAD.   ITALIAN SALAD.

FRUIT JELLY.   LIQUEUR JELLY.   MERINGUE CREAM.

CHEESE AND BISCUITS.

COFFEE   DESSERT.

The menu of the celebratory lunch at the opening of Lever Park in May 1904.

The Recreation Ground, off Longsight, Harwood.
The land was given by Robert Bolton.

very often, the family from Ireland became regular visitors and the Scowcrofts of Bradshaw made many journeys to Ireland. Samuel was in his element as he could now sail as often as he wished to see his daughter, son-in-law and granddaughter. Edith would never be lonely as her brothers, wives, children and aunts made frequent visits.

On one of Samuel's many visits to Ireland there was an accident on the railway causing his train to be delayed and miss the boat from Heysham. The train was then diverted via Carlisle to Stranraer where they boarded the ship for Larne. This was the shortest and roughest crossing where the Irish Sea meets the Atlantic Ocean in the North Channel. Folklore has it that the giants who had missed the stepping-stones fought beneath the waves to create these mighty seas. Samuel would stride the deck enjoying every moment whilst his wife would be lying in a cabin feeling rather seasick. Whilst in Ireland Samuel visited many places of interest; his energy was boundless, he used all the local means of transport – trams, horse tramcars and jaunty cars,. On one visit they watched the Orange Parade through Belfast that is still organised to this day. Samuel was beginning to think Ireland was better than Scotland. It was during this time that he became very friendly with Captain Hill, the captain of one of the boats crossing the Irish Sea, and on his retirement they visited many places of interest together including shipyards in Ireland and England.

Presentation of Gifts

On August 25th 1906 at Harwood Wesleyan School the trustees presented Robert Bolton, Samuel's cousin, and Joseph Bolton, Robert's son, with a silver rose bowl each and Major Hardcastle with a pair of silver vases in appreciation of their gifts to Harwood. These included land from Robert Bolton for the recreation ground, from Joseph Bolton for the burial ground and from Major Hardcastle for the school site. A silver mounted walking stick was presented to Samuel for of his services to the community.

After this presentation, Samuel, Lizzie and Edwin went off again to Belfast for another three weeks holiday. Samuel and Edwin couldn't resist another visit to Giant's Causeway although it was a journey of 140 miles and cost of 2s 6d. He took Lizzie to visit gardens full of apple and pear trees, picked pounds of blackberries and returned to Bradshaw full of renewed energy. On 9th November Samuel watched the demolition of the cottages next to the smithy, formerly the old factory on Lea Gate. A new till was needed for the shop, so Samuel purchased a National Till at a cost of £38 to make the reckoning a little easier. Arthur, Edith and Evelyn came to Bradshaw for Christmas and the usual 'Conversazione' at the chapel. On New Year's Day 1907, Samuel took them all to the Victoria Hall, Bolton to see a cinematograph show given by Mr Hibbert;

A party of Longsight Methodists filling in ponds at the old Brick Works. This was part of the land given by Thomas Hardcastle, now used by the Manse and Tennis Club, c.1909.

The Longsight Methodist Men's Class, c.1910.

which would be the highlight of their visit. Another significant event occurred when Samuel was invited to attend the opening of the King's Hall, Bolton on February 6th 1907.

There had been a number of burglaries in the area and Samuel, conscious of the need for security in his stores, had iron bars fitted to his drapery shop window to deter intruders including rampaging cows that had caused trouble previously .

Samuel and Lizzie were very sociable and on 16th February they were invited to the diamond wedding celebration of Mr and Mrs Richard Wild. There were 160 guests at the party held at Bradshaw School (now converted into The Old School House Restaurant). Samuel was still in great demand for committees and at the April meeting of the Board of Guardians he was appointed a Day School Manager. As the T.U.D.C. representative for Bradshaw Church School he attended his first meeting two weeks later in May.

Samuel junior wasn't feeling too well and money not being a problem, a voyage to Canada was organised to speed his recovery. Samuel, Lizzie, Peter Alfred, his wife and Samuel's granddaughter Lizzie went to Liverpool to see the SS Tusania on which Samuel junior would be sailing. The next day on August 22nd 1907 he embarked with two friends and sailed for Montreal; as they were nearing Quebec a bridge which was under construction collapsed and seventy people drowned. Fortunately the Tusania missed this accident. A cablegram was sent to Bradshaw to say they had arrived safely in Quebec after an eight-day voyage. Samuel junior returned from Canada on the Ivernia to Liverpool after a five-week holiday, his friends returning two weeks later. Samuel had fully recovered and was ready for business.

Bolton Holidays

Bolton holidays started on August 19th 1907 when the mills had a week's holiday and the shops closed for two days. Samuel waited until September, when it was his 69th birthday, to take his wife Lizzie to St Annes. Not quite as exciting as their son going to Canada, but they managed to include a few boat trips. They returned home for the visit of their daughter and family from Belfast. After a three-day stay Samuel and Lizzie returned with them to Belfast. Portrush and the Giant's Causeway was again on the agenda as was Comber Fair in Belfast where they saw the Viceroy and his Lady. His son-in-law, Arthur, bought the villa next door to the house at Knock probably to accommodate the visitors from Bradshaw. Samuel and Lizzie again went to Ireland for Christmas.

On March 8th 1908, Samuel Junior's wife, Annie, gave birth to a baby girl, Elsie, who was born at their home, 30 Church Street, Harwood, another granddaughter for Samuel to spoil.

On the last week of June 1908 when Bolton and District holidays were arranged for the second year, the mills and factories closed for a week and the shops for a few days. These fixed holidays continued until recent times when supermarkets and the decline of the textile industry made them redundant.

Whilst reading Samuel's diary one gets the impression that he was never still and always organising the church, his business, or holidays. Once, on a free day, he took Lizzie out. They rode on the tram to Bolton, then to Bury and Rawtenstall by rail, then tram to Haslingden, Accrington and Blackburn, returning by rail to Bolton and tram to Bradshaw Brow before stretching their legs on the walk back to Bradshaw Chapel. After this it was back to everyday duties like making sure the urinals near the Schoolhouse, Bradshaw Chapel were completed satisfactorily, then confirming that the wayside seat had been moved from Lee Gate to Bradshaw Road as no one would wish to sit for a rest near the toilets. All this happened in the year of Samuel's 70th birthday.

Retirement

Coming up to his 70th birthday Samuel decided it was time to buy a house for retirement so he treated himself to No 59 Longsight, Harwood; the price was not recorded. Robert Bolton who owned land near the recreation ground, part of Posey Bank Farm, allowed him a piece of land for a garden on which Samuel employed 8 men to clear the ground, turn the sods and complete the fencing. After buying his new home, Samuel sent notification to Tom Scowcroft of Tonge Colliery and owner of 76 Bradshaw Chapel, that he was going to move and on 30th March 1909 returned from Belfast to live at the new home. He made arrangements with Tom Scowcroft to continue to rent stables and a coach house for £4 a year. He left the rose trees, sold surplus furniture, returned the keys and said goodbye to No 76. Whilst he was on holiday in Belfast, his sons made a doorway from the Bradshaw Road shop into the bottom warehouse. His sons were obviously as capable of running a successful business as Samuel.

Old Age Pensions Paid

On 1st January 1909 the first payment of the national old age pension was made, which was a great relief to many people otherwise without means of support. Samuel was still a very active member of the Turton Urban District Council and was re-elected as guardian for Bradshaw and appointed chairman of the stores sub committee at Fishpool Workhouse at Farnworth.

The Manufacture of Sanoper

Samuel's sons Samuel junior and Peter Alfred were very interested in selling a scouring powder called Sanoper which was prepared in Australia. After several meetings with Mr Pearson, their contact in the firm, they entertained him in London and Blackpool to persuade him that they should sell the product. Mr Pearson and family were even taken to France for a few days but nothing positive was achieved. Finally in February 1910 they met again in Birmingham and finalised the deal. The name Sanoper was an anagram of Pearson.

On reaching the age of 71, Samuel was presented with a diploma and badge for his 25 years service as Librarian at Harwood School.

Opening of the Barlow Institute

Even in his 72nd year, Samuel was still an active figure in Bradshaw. On 30th October 1909 he and his wife were invited to the opening of the Barlow Institute and were greeted there by Sir Thomas Barlow. The Institute was presented to the villagers of Edgworth by Sir Thomas and his sister Annie as a place for meetings and entertainment. To this day it is still used for the same purposes plus a computer room.

Another invitation on 16th March 1910 was to the opening of Wilkinson's Sanatorium at Sweetloves, a gift from Thomas Wilkinson. It was demolished a few years ago and replaced by a housing estate, 'The Beeches', which, on the site of a sanatorium, is still supposed to be a healthy place to live.

Meanwhile, at 59 Longsight when Samuel was digging in his garden he found a spring which saved him carrying water for his plants. During this period, whilst Samuel was enjoying the delights of his garden, his sons were preparing the top warehouse at Bradshaw Road by dividing it and preparing space for a machine to make metal polish, which they named 'Three Nines'. A large foundation stone was purchased from Cox Green Quarry, Egerton for the engine bed and a new gas engine fixed into place under the warehouse making everything ready for manufacturing.

Samuel also received visits from his other relations; on one occasion Joseph Scowcroft from Ogden, Utah, U.S.A arrived in England. He called on Samuel and Lizzie in his motorcar, which would certainly bring the neighbours out in 1910. He took Samuel and Lizzie on a visit to Hall i'th' Wood, Smithills Hall, Turton Tower and Harwood Wesleyan Chapel. Next day Joseph, his wife, son and daughter called again for dinner and tea, making sure that everyone had seen his car. Would Samuel be envious or would he be thinking that he preferred his faithful horse and cart?

Back Bradshaw Road – where Samuel stabled his horses.

The basement and extension to the new shop on Bradshaw Road.

No 59 Longsight, the house Samuel bought on his retirement in 1909.

1908   <u>164</u>

Decr 19   Edward Hindle (Lawrence son) buried at Bradshaw Ch

20   Went to reopening of Knock presbyterian ch   professor Heron. Dr ch Rev

28   Earthquake in Messina   dreadful loss of life as well as shipping

29   Robert Allen 2nd wife died at Bradshaw Brow aged 49

31   Heavy snow at Knock   In Scotland trains were snowed up for 28 h^{rs}

1909

Jany 1   R B & P A and wife came to Knock to see us. crossed on the Antrim.

1   The first payments of old age pensions this day

4   R B. P A & Annie ret. from Knock via Heysham on Antrim home.

9   Mary Brooks (West Scowcroft, daughter Holmes) died at Cockey moor aged 60

13   Alex^r Kilburn choked with some mutton at Kershaws beershop up Bru

14   Rev^d A Stephens vicar of Brightmet died aged 65

19   Robert Allen died at Bradshaw Brow aged 59   ~~was~~ buried Brad Ch.

19   Robert Riley died (Johns son) at Longsight aged 59

23   Loss of the SS Republic - Wireless message first used six s to s to

     ↓ her assistance

30   John Nunderdale died - P A wife bro in Law - buried Feb 2

Feby 12   Edward Holt . Brownhill farm. Died in his 72 year

15   Jane Fish   Jesse widow died Turton Lane

17   Catherine Connell died in Fishpool workhouse aged 103 years

20   Joseph Tootle died at Egerton Road Southport buried M^r son 23

25   Went with Captⁿ Hill to Harland & Wolfe shipyard

25   P A and wife went to London. ret^d on March 2nd

March 11   Wm Porritt Harwood Lodge died aged 74   Was buried

     at Farnworth cemetery

17   Large fire at Messrs Deakins works Belmont

29   Left Knock. Belfast for home on Antrim capⁿ Hill.

*Dec 1908 – Mar 1909. Entries include notes on Irish holidays, including a
visit to Harland & Wolfe Shipyard with Captain Hill.*

Barlow Institute, Edgworth: Samuel and Lizzie were invited to the official opening in 1909.

Wilkinson Sanatorium, Sharples: another grand opening to which Samuel Scowcroft was invited in 1910.

Samuel took up gardening very seriously by growing sweet peas and roses of all varieties in summer and chrysanthemums in the autumn. In the vegetable garden he had a strawberry patch, peas, apples, loganberries, black currants and red currants. Many of his friends came to admire his garden and to sit and chat in the peaceful surroundings. His nephew, Edwin Scowcroft also had a garden in Harwood and they would exchange plants.

Samuel finished his diaries in 1910. He collected entries from notebooks and pieces of paper and wrote up two separate copies in a very neat hand. One went to his granddaughter Mary Olivia Scowcroft of Lee Gate whose copy has been used for this publication. The other is owned by Sheila Scowcroft of Wakefield who inherited it from Elsie Ormrod Barker, a granddaughter of Samuel.

During his years of retirement Samuel continued to travel to Ireland for holidays. In 1913 all the family came together for the wedding of his son Robert Bolton to Ellen Pilling of Lee Gate Farm (the parents of Mary Scowcroft). A sad occasion occurred in 1913 when Samuel's wife Lizzie died aged 72 years after 48 wonderful years of marriage. The following August, Samuel himself died just before his 76th birthday at his daughter's house, 4 Villiers Road, Rathgar, Dublin. His body was brought back to Bradshaw Church where he was buried alongside his wife on 8th August 1914.

The descendants of Samuel Scowcroft must be very proud of his lifetime achievements and how Harwood and Bradshaw benefited from his careful, watchful eye. He made improvements to Harwood Wesleyan Chapel, to Bradshaw Church and to both their schools. He ran a successful business and still found time to be caring for the sick and poor; a man who must surely have been missed by everyone.

190

Mr

Bought of Samuel Scowcroft,

Supply Stores, Bradshaw Chapel, near Bolton.
The corner Shop, 1 Turton Road.
The White Shop, 53 Tonge Moor Road.

An early 1900's billhead of Samuel Scowcroft detailing his three stores.

*Group of
Longsight
Methodists
on a summer
outing,
c.1909*

*A Longsight
Methodist outing to
Asmus Fold Farm,
c.1909*

*A Longsight
Methodist
Field Day at
Springside
Farm (now
the site of
Bramdean
Estate):
c.1920.*